Earth Science

Directed Reading
Worksheets

HOLT, RINEHART AND WINSTON

A Harcourt Classroom Education Company

Austin • New York • Orlando • Atlanta • San Francisco • Boston • Dallas • Toronto • London

Welcome!

Imagine that you have just entered a foreign land and encountered a unique culture. What better way to experience the unfamiliar territory than to find a knowledgeable guide? He or she could point out beautiful landscapes and historical landmarks while dazzling you with interesting tidbits about the region. Your guide could help you make the most of your visit and help make it a visit you'll remember.

Well you have just entered a foreign realm! You've entered the world of *Holt Science & Technology Earth Science.* To help you make the most of your journey, use this booklet as your personal guide. Your guide will help you focus your attention on interesting images and important scientific facts. Your guide will also offer tips to help you understand the local language and ask you questions along the way to make sure you don't miss anything.

So sit back and get ready to fully experience *Holt Science & Technology!* Don't worry, this guide knows the ropes—all you have to do is follow along!

Art and Photo Credits
All work, unless otherwise noted, contributed by Holt, Rinehart and Winston.
Abbreviated as follows: (t) top; (b) bottom; (l) left; (r) right; (c) center; (bkgd) background.
Front cover (owl), Kim Taylor/Bruce Coleman, Inc.; (fossil), Barry Rosenthal/FPG International; (fault), David Parker/Science Photo Library/Photo Researchers, Inc.; Page 54 (b), David Chapman; 57 (t), Carlyn Iverson; 58 (c), Carlyn Iverson

Printed in the United States of America

ISBN 0-03-054387-8   3 4 5 6   085   04 03 02 01

▪ CONTENTS ▪

Chapter 1: The World of Earth Science 1

Chapter 2: Maps as Models of the Earth 9

Chapter 3: Minerals of the Earth's Crust 15

Chapter 4: Rocks: Mineral Mixtures 21

Chapter 5: Energy Resources 29

Chapter 6: The Rock and Fossil Record 37

Chapter 7: Plate Tectonics 49

Chapter 8: Earthquakes 59

Chapter 9: Volcanoes 67

Chapter 10: Weathering and Soil Formation 75

Chapter 11: The Flow of Fresh Water 83

Chapter 12: Agents of Erosion and Deposition 91

Chapter 13: Exploring the Oceans 101

Chapter 14: The Movement of Ocean Water 113

Chapter 15: The Atmosphere 121

Chapter 16: Understanding Weather 129

Chapter 17: Climate 137

Chapter 18: Observing the Sky 145

Chapter 19: Formation of the Solar System 153

Chapter 20: A Family of Planets 163

Chapter 21: The Universe Beyond 171

Chapter 22: Exploring Space 179

Name _____ Date _____ Class _____

DIRECTED READING WORKSHEET

The World of Earth Science

As you read Chapter 1, which begins on page 4 of your textbook, answer the following questions.

This Really Happened! (p. 4)

1. How did the hikers behave like Earth scientists?

_____

_____

_____

_____

_____

What Do You Think? (p. 5)

Answer these questions in your ScienceLog now. Then later, you'll have a chance to revise your answers based on what you've learned.

Investigate! (p. 5)

2. What is the purpose of this activity?

_____

_____

_____

Section 1: Branches of Earth Science (p. 6)

3. The study of the physical planet Earth is divided into

_____ , _____ , and

_____ . The study of all physical things

beyond planet Earth is _____ .

Geology—Science that Rocks (p. 6)

Choose the kind of geologist in Column B that you would most likely find at each of the sites in Column A, and write the corresponding letter in the appropriate space.

Column A	Column B
_____ **4.** a volcano in Hawaii	**a.** seismologist
_____ **5.** an earthquake site in California	**b.** paleontologist
_____ **6.** a canyon containing fossilized animal bones	**c.** volcanologist

7. What geologic evidence tells Robert Fronk that sea level was once much lower than it is now?

_____

_____

_____

_____

Oceanography—Water, Water Everywhere (p. 7)

8. How do biological communities around *black smokers* survive?

_____

_____

_____

_____

Meteorology—It's a Gas! (p. 8)

9. Meteorology is the study of the _____ .

10. Did meteorologists help save people's lives when Hurricane Andrew hit Florida? Explain.

_____

_____

_____

_____

11. Why do scientists like Howard Bluestein chase tornadoes? (Circle all that apply.)

  a. to learn more about them
  b. to learn more about earthquakes
  c. to try to stop them
  d. to learn how to predict tornado behavior

Astronomy—Far, Far Away (p. 9)

12. Give three examples of the "physical things beyond Earth" that astronomers might study.

  _____

  _____

13. Galileo built a radio telescope in 1609. True or False? (Circle one.)

14. The closest star to Earth is _____ .

Special Branches of Earth Science (p. 10)

15. What is an ecosystem?

  _____

  _____

After reading pages 10 and 11, choose the kind of Earth scientist in Column B that best matches the description in Column A, and write the corresponding letter in the appropriate space.

Column A	Column B
_____ **16.** studies the Earth's surface features	**a.** cartographer
_____ **17.** studies the relationship between organisms and their surroundings	**b.** geographer
_____ **18.** studies the relationship between humans and their surroundings	**c.** environmental scientist
_____ **19.** makes maps of the Earth's surface features	**d.** geochemist
_____ **20.** studies the chemistry of soil, rocks, and minerals	**e.** ecologist

Review (p. 11)

Now that you've finished Section 1, review what you learned by answering the Review questions in your ScienceLog.

Section 2: The Scientific Method in Earth Science (p. 12)

1. What is causing the booming and the tremors in the description at the beginning of Section 2?

_____

_____

_____

Steps of the Scientific Method (p. 13)

2. The goal of the scientific method is to
   a. solve problems by guessing.
   b. find answers in science books.
   c. reach reliable answers and solutions.
   d. help scientists take shortcuts during research.

3. Look at the flowchart in Figure 10. If the conclusions that you draw do not fit your hypothesis, what are three things that you might do next?

_____

_____

_____

Dino Discovery—A Case for the Scientific Method (p. 14)

Given below in Column A are descriptions of tasks that Dr. Gillette performed in his scientific investigation. Choose the step of the scientific method in Column B that best matches the description in Column A, and write the corresponding letter in the space provided.

Column A	Column B
_____ 4. found the bones were too large or too differently shaped to come from any known dinosaur	a. Ask a question.
_____ 5. concluded that the bones belonged to a newly discovered type of dinosaur	b. Form a hypothesis.
_____ 6. measured the bones and compared them with known dinosaurs' bones	c. Test the hypothesis.
_____ 7. wondered what type of dinosaur the bones came from	d. Analyze the results.
_____ 8. thought the bones possibly came from a dinosaur unknown to science	e. Draw conclusions.

_____

Chapter 1, continued

Case Closed? (p. 17)

9. Was Dr. Gillette's work on the *Seismosaurus hallorum* finished after he communicated his results? Explain.

_____

_____

_____

Review (p. 17)

Now that you've finished Section 2, review what you learned by answering the Review questions in your ScienceLog.

Section 3: Life in a Warmer World—An Earth Science Model (p. 18)

1. All scientists believe that the world is getting dangerously warm.

True or False? (Circle one.)

Using the information in Figure 13, choose the outcome in Column B that is a direct result of the occurrence in Column A, and write the corresponding letter in the space provided.

Column A	Column B
____ **2.** volume of oceans expand	**a.** flooding and loss of fertile soil
____ **3.** more evaporation from oceans, lakes, and streams	**b.** sea level rises
____ **4.** increased rain	**c.** increased water vapor in atmosphere

Types of Scientific Models (p. 19)

5. List two ways that models are useful to scientists.

_____

_____

_____

6. Engineers test airplane models in wind tunnels for all of the following reasons EXCEPT

    a. to see how aerodynamic they are.
    b. because it is safer to test models than a real airplane.
    c. because it is less expensive to discover problems with models than with a real airplane.
    d. to find out how airplanes deflect radiation.

Chapter 1, continued

---

7. A unifying _____ for a broad range of hypotheses and observations that have been supported

by _____ is called a theory.

The Global-Warming Model (p. 20)

8. Take a moment to look at the Environment Connection. When the amount of carbon dioxide in the atmosphere increases, the

greenhouse effect _____ .

9. Read page 20 and then look at Figure 16. What do greenhouse gases do?

_____

_____

_____

Testing the Global-Warming Model (p. 20)

10. Scientists can test the global-warming model by

   a. ignoring data.
   b. seeing how accurately the model explains Earth's climate.
   c. comparing the Earth's weather with the weather on Venus.

11. Scientists have been successful in predicting the actual amount

of global warming during the last century. True or False? (Circle one.)

Using the Global-Warming Model (p. 21)

12. Why can't scientists claim 100 percent accuracy when making predictions based on the global-warming climate model?

_____

_____

_____

_____

_____

Review (p. 21)

Now that you've finished Section 3, review what you learned by answering the Review questions in your ScienceLog.

_____
Chapter 1, continued

Section 4: Measurement and Safety (p. 22)

1. At one time in England what was the standard for an inch?

_____

_____

2. Why was the International System of Units developed?

_____

_____

_____

Using the SI System (p. 22)

3. Name one advantage of using SI measurements over the English system.

_____

_____

_____

4. After reviewing Figure 17, try the following problem: Imagine that a hurricane has just caused a lot of damage in Coastville. An amateur group of meteorologists have asked you to help with the damage assessment, but they do not understand the SI system. Help them by filling in the measurement needed for each damage scenario. In the third column, fill in the appropriate SI unit of measurement to use.

Damage	Measurement	SI unit
height of a tree uprooted in the storm		
the amount of water in a flooded garage	volume	
amount of matter blocking a doorway		kilogram (kg)
amount of rainwater collected in a cylinder		
a flood victim's fever		

Chapter 1, continued

5. Volume is described on pages 23 and 24. What is one way to measure the volume of an irregularly shaped object?

_____

_____

_____

_____

_____

_____

6. Temperature is described on page 25. Normal body temperature in

degrees Celsius is _____ .

Safety Rules! (p. 25)

7. Write in the description for each safety symbol in the chart below.

Review (p. 25)

Now that you've finished Section 4, review what you learned by answering the Review questions in your ScienceLog.

CHAPTER

2 **DIRECTED READING WORKSHEET**

Maps as Models of the Earth

As you read Chapter 2, which begins on page 32 of your textbook, answer the following questions.

Imagine . . . (p. 32)

1. Before paper was used, how did people make maps?

_____

_____

_____

What Do You Think? (p. 33)

Answer these questions in your ScienceLog now. Then later, you'll have a chance to revise your answers based on what you've learned.

Investigate! (p. 33)

2. What two things will you do in this activity?

_____

_____

Section 1: You Are Here (p. 34)

3. How is the map in Figure 1 different from one you might see today?

_____

_____

_____

What Does the Earth Really Look Like? (p. 34)

Mark each of the following statements *True* or *False*.

4. _____ Christopher Columbus was the first person to think that the Earth was shaped like a sphere.

5. _____ More than 2,000 years ago, Eratosthenes calculated the Earth's circumference with an error of only 15 percent.

Chapter 2, continued

Finding Direction on Earth (p. 35)

6. Because the Earth is a sphere, we describe direction and location on Earth using _____ as reference points. (Circle one.)

   a. the North and South Poles   **c.** the stars
   b. the West and East Poles   **d.** None of the above

7. Label the following directions on the diagram: south, southwest, east, northwest, west, southeast, northeast.

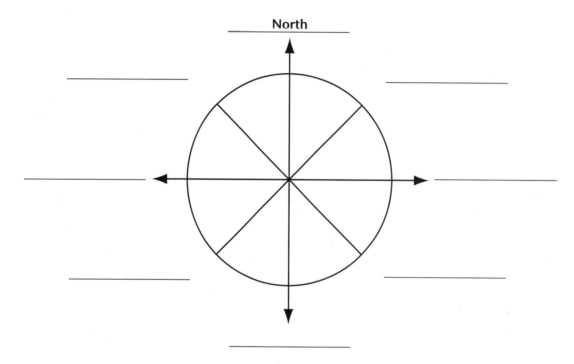

8. Magnetic poles and geographic poles are at different locations on the Earth. True or False? (Circle one.)

9. Which kind of pole is true north?

   a. a geologic pole   **c.** a magnetic pole
   b. a geographic pole   **d.** None of the above

10. In order to find true north with a compass, you must use an angle of correction called _____.

11. Take a moment to read the Astronomy Connection in the right column on page 37. If you point your right hand in the direction that the sun rises in the morning, in what direction would you point your left hand so that you face north?

   a. north   **c.** west
   b. south   **d.** east

Chapter 2, continued

Finding Locations on the Earth (p. 37)

12. Latitude and longitude are used in combination to create

_____ addresses.

Mark each of the following statements *True* or *False*.

13. _____ Imaginary lines drawn parallel to the equator are called lines of longitude.

14. _____ The equator divides the Earth into the Western and Eastern Hemispheres.

15. _____ All lines of longitude intersect at only two points.

16. _____ Lines of latitude sometimes intersect.

17. The prime meridian
  a. circles the globe like the equator.
  b. runs from the North Pole to the South Pole.
  c. was set at 180° through an international agreement.

18. In Figure 8 on page 39, what line of latitude runs just north of Springfield, Illinois?

_____

19. What line of longitude runs just west of Springfield, Illinois?

_____

Review (p. 39)

Now that you've finished Section 1, review what you learned by answering the Review questions in your ScienceLog.

Section 2: Mapping the Earth's Surface (p. 40)

1. Why it is better to use a map than a globe when studying the Earth's surface? (Circle all that apply.)
  a. Maps show more detail than globes.
  b. Maps can show all of the Earth or a part of it.
  c. Maps are the most accurate models of the Earth.

A Flat Sphere? (p. 40)

2. Changes in the shapes and sizes of land features and oceans caused by transferring information from a globe to a flat map are

called _____ .

3. Name three geometric shapes on which mapmakers base map projections.

_____

_____

Chapter 2, continued

_____

After you finish reading pages 41–42, label each of the following as a feature of a Mercator, conic, or azimuthal projection. Write *M* for Mercator, *C* for conic, or *A* for azimuthal.

4. _____ Area of decreased distortion is around only one point.

5. _____ It's best for mapping land masses that have more area east to west than north to south.

6. _____ It has great distortion around the poles.

7. _____ Lines of latitude are parallel, and lines of longitude are parallel as well.

8. _____ It has no distortion along one line of latitude.

Modern Mapmaking (p. 43)

9. How have airplanes had an effect on mapmaking?

_____

_____

_____

_____

10. A bird's-eye view of the Earth photographed by a camera on a plane is called

a. a satellite image.   **c.** an aerial photograph.
b. a Mercator projection.   **d.** None of the above

11. If a scientist collected data about an object while being near the

object, we say the scientist used remote sensing. True or False? (Circle one.)

12. Give two examples of tools used in remote sensing.

_____

_____

_____

13. Satellites collect information about energy coming from the

Earth's surface. True or False? (Circle one.)

Information Shown on Maps (p. 44)

Use Figure 14 to answer the following questions.

14. The part of a map that gives a list of symbols and their

explanations is a _____ .

15. The subject of the map is given in the _____ .

16. The _____ scale can be used to measure distance on a map.

17. The proportional, unitless relationship between a distance on the map and the distance on the Earth's surface is called

the _____ .

Review (p. 45)

Now that you've finished Section 2, review what you learned by answering the Review questions in your ScienceLog.

Section 3: Topographic Maps (p. 46)

1. A topographic map would be the best kind of map to use on

a. a sea cruise.   **c.** a trip to the moon.
b. a tour of Manhattan.   **d.** an outdoor adventure trip.

2. A topographic map shows only natural features, such as rivers,

lakes, and mountains. True or False? (Circle one.)

Elements of Elevation (p. 46)

3. What government agency has made topographic maps for all of the United States? Write out the full name and the abbreviation.

_____

4. In Figure 15, each contour line connects points with the same

_____ .

5. Suppose you are looking at a map that has a small contour interval. What might this tell you about the land?

a. It is mountainous.   **c.** It has high relief.
b. It is relatively flat.   **d.** It has steep slopes.

6. If you are hiking on a trail with a steep slope, the contour lines

on your map will be close together. True or False? (Circle one.)

7. The index contour is _____ than the other

contour lines, and is labeled by _____ .
(heavier or lighter, slope or elevation)

Chapter 2, continued

Reading a Topographic Map (p. 48)

Write the color that indicates each feature on a topographic map.

8. Wooded areas are shaded _____ .

9. Contour lines are _____ .

10. Roads, bridges, and railroads are drawn in

_____ .

11. Major highways are colored _____ .

Take a look at the legend in Figure 17. Then choose the symbol in Column B that best matches the description in Column A, and write the corresponding letter in the space provided.

Column A	Column B
____ **12.** a school building	**a.**
____ **13.** a bridge	**b.**
____ **14.** a swamp	**c.**
____ **15.** a railroad track	**d.**

16. Why might the Texas Parks and Wildlife Department use a topographic map?

    a. to look for a street address
    b. to keep track of active volcanoes
    c. to protect the habitats of endangered species
    d. They never use topographic maps.

17. What does a V-shaped contour line mean?

_____

18. Describe a depression on a contour map.

_____

_____

Review (p. 49)

Now that you've finished Section 3, review what you learned by answering the Review questions in your ScienceLog.

CHAPTER

3 **DIRECTED READING WORKSHEET**

Minerals of the Earth's Crust

As you read Chapter 3, which begins on page 58 of your textbook, answer the following questions.

Imagine . . . (p. 58)

1. Rubies, sandpaper, and sapphires have a connection. What is it?

_____

_____

_____

2. Gems aren't valuable because of the elements they're made of. Why are they so valuable?

_____

_____

_____

What Do You Think? (p. 59)

Answer these questions in your ScienceLog now. Then later, you'll have a chance to revise your answers based on what you've learned.

Investigate! (p. 59)

3. In this activity, materials are classified as _____

or as _____ .

Section 1: What Is a Mineral? (p. 60)

4. Which of the following are characteristics of a mineral? (Circle all that apply.)

a. It can be made in a laboratory.
b. It is nonliving material.
c. It is a liquid or a gas.
d. It has a repeating inner structure.

Minerals: From the Inside Out (p. 60)

Use the information on pages 60–61 to choose the term in Column B that best matches the description in Column A, and write the corresponding letter in the space provided.

Column A	Column B
____ **5.** smallest part of an element that has all the properties of that element	**a.** crystal
____ **6.** substance that cannot be chemically broken down into a simpler form	**b.** atom
____ **7.** formed when the atoms of two or more elements bond together chemically	**c.** element
____ **8.** solid, geometric form of a mineral produced by a repeating pattern of atoms	**d.** compound

9. Which of the following is NOT a characteristic of a crystal?

  a. The arrangement of the atoms in a crystal determines its shape.

  b. The arrangement of the atoms in a crystal is determined by the atoms that make up the mineral.

  c. A crystalline structure is always geometric.

  d. Crystals are classified according to their mineral content.

Types of Minerals (p. 62)

10. Minerals are commonly classified by _____ composition.

11. Take a moment to read the Biology Connection on page 62. A mineral found in the brain of certain fish gives the fish a sense

of direction. True or False? (Circle one.)

12. Silicate minerals contain _____ and

_____, the two most common elements in the Earth's crust.

13. All silicate minerals contain iron. True or False? (Circle one.)

14. Look at Figure 3. What minerals are included in the composition of this piece of granite?

_____

_____

_____

Chapter 3, continued

Choose the type of nonsilicate mineral in Column B that best matches the clue in Column A, and write the corresponding letter in the space provided. You may use items in Column B more than once.

Column A	Column B
____ **15.** used to make toothpaste	**a.** native elements
____ **16.** diamond, for example	**b.** carbonates
____ **17.** used to make medicines	**c.** halides
____ **18.** rock salt, for example	**d.** oxides
____ **19.** used to make fireworks	**e.** sulfates
____ **20.** used to make aircraft parts	**f.** sulfides
____ **21.** used to make fertilizer	
____ **22.** contain only one element	

Review (p. 63)

Now that you've finished Section 1, review what you learned by answering the Review questions in your ScienceLog.

Section 2: Identifying Minerals (p. 64)

1. What do the two mineral samples pictured at the top of page 64 have in common?

_____

_____

_____

Color (p. 64)

2. Amethyst, a variety of quartz, is purple because it contains certain

kinds of _____ .

3. Suppose you found a golden mineral. Could you tell if it was pyrite by its color? Why or why not?

_____

_____

_____

CHAPTER 3

Luster (p. 64)

4. Luster is the way a surface reflects _____ .

5. Suppose you find a mineral on the way to school. You notice that it looks greasy and oily in light. How would you classify it according to the Luster Chart on page 64?

_____

_____

_____

Streak (p. 65)

6. The mark a mineral leaves on a piece of unglazed porcelain,

   called a _____ , is the mineral's streak.

7. When a mineral's color is changed by weathering, its streak also

   changes. True or False? (Circle one.)

Cleavage and Fracture (p. 65)

8. A gem cutter uses a mineral's natural _____
   to remove flaws from diamonds and rubies.

9. Cleavage and fracture both describe the way minerals break. How are cleavage and fracture different?

_____

_____

_____

_____

10. A curved fracture pattern is called a(n)
    a. elliptical fracture.
    b. circular fracture.
    c. conchoidal fracture.
    d. bending fracture.

Hardness (p. 66)

11. A mineral's hardness can be determined by scratching its surface

    with the 10 reference minerals. True or False? (Circle one.)

12. Suppose you find a mineral that scratches calcite, is scratched by corundum, does not scratch topaz, and scratches quartz. What is this mineral's hardness on the Mohs' scale picture on page 66?

_____

_____

Density (p. 66)

13. A golf ball feels heavier than a table-tennis ball because the golf

ball has a _____ density.
(greater or lower)

14. Specific gravity is the ratio of an object's density to that of

_____ .

Special Properties (p. 67)

15. To test a mineral for _____ , I would use
an ultraviolet light. To test a mineral for radioactivity, I would use

_____ .

Review (p. 67)

Now that you've finished Section 2, review what you learned by answering the Review questions in your ScienceLog.

Section 3: The Formation and Mining of Minerals (p. 68)

Pages 68–69 show how minerals form. Choose the mineral in Column B that best matches the description in Column A, and write the corresponding letter in the space provided.

Column A	Column B
_____ **1.** forms from slowly cooled magma that solidifies into a pluton	**a.** gold
_____ **2.** forms when a body of salt water evaporates	**b.** garnet
_____ **3.** crystallizes out of ground water that has been heated by magma	**c.** feldspar
_____ **4.** forms in tear-shaped pegmatites in the presence of hot fluids	**d.** gypsum
_____ **5.** forms in metamorphic rock	**e.** calcite
_____ **6.** forms from materials dissolved in water that eventually crystalize	**f.** topaz

---

Mining (p. 70)

Use the text and illustrations on page 70 to answer the following questions.

7. Suppose you see a miner working in an open pit mine. What minerals might the miner be mining?

_____

_____

8. The method commonly used to mine diamond is called

_____ .

The Value of Minerals (p. 71)

9. Suppose you had an airplane factory and you needed more beryllium. Which mineral would you need to mine to get the beryllium?

_____

10. Which of the following are common uses for chromium? (Circle all that apply.)

a. making coins   **c.** making stainless steel
b. making batteries   **d.** making cast iron

11. Mineral crystals that are attractive and rare are called

_____ .

Responsible Mining (p. 71)

12. Reclamation helps reduce the harmful effects of mining. What are two problems with reclamation?

_____

_____

_____

13. How can we reduce our need for mineral ore?

_____

_____

Review (p. 71)

Now that you've finished Section 3, review what you learned by answering the Review questions in your ScienceLog.

CHAPTER

4 **DIRECTED READING WORKSHEET**

Rocks: Mineral Mixtures

As you read Chapter 4, which begins on page 78 of your textbook, answer the following questions.

Imagine . . . (p. 78)

Mark each of the following statements *True* or *False*.

1. The sandstone of the Red Rocks Amphitheater took 12 million years to form. True or False? (Circle one.)

2. The Red Rocks Amphitheater is a structure built entirely by humans. True or False? (Circle one.)

What Do You Think? (p. 79)

Answer these questions in your ScienceLog now. Then later, you'll have a chance to revise your answers based on what you've learned.

Investigate! (p. 79)

3. In this activity, which material is used to represent the three rock types?
   - **a.** silly putty
   - **b.** modeling clay
   - **c.** glue
   - **d.** gum

Section 1: Understanding Rock (p. 80)

4. Rock is a solid _____ of crystals of one or more minerals.

The Value of Rock (p. 80)

5. How is the scalpel shown in Figure 2, on page 80, similar to stone tools used by early humans?

   _____

   _____

   _____

6. Which of the following rocks have been used as building materials? (Circle all that apply.)
   - **a.** marble
   - **b.** obsidian
   - **c.** limestone
   - **d.** slate

7. Fossils found in rocks provide clues about the history of

   _____ on Earth.

The Rock Cycle (p. 82)

8. Scientists classify rocks into one of the three main categories by

   a. what they look like.

   b. what they are made of.

   c. how they are broken down.

   d. how they form.

Use the diagram on pages 82 and 83 to answer questions 9–13.

9. Which of the following is NOT one of the main types of rock?

   a. sedimentary   **c.** igneous

   b. tertiary   **d.** metamorphic

10. Grains of sand are _____ from mountains and wash down in rivers to the sea.

11. Which kind of rock could be described as being formed by "pressure cooking"?

_____

_____

12. What processes transform magma into igneous rock? (Circle all that apply.)

   a. cooling   **c.** solidification

   b. melting   **d.** evaporating

13. Sedimentary rock forms from the cooling of magma.

   True or False? (Circle one.)

14. Look at Figure 5 on page 84. The sediments that form sedimentary rock can come only from metamorphic rock. True or False? (Circle one.)

15. Figure 5 shows that heat and pressure will change igneous rock into _____ rock.

The Nitty-Gritty on Rock Classification (p. 85)

16. Earth scientists classify different rocks according to their

_____ and their

_____ .

17. What determines the composition of a rock?

_____

_____

Chapter 4, continued

---

18. Small-grained rocks have a _____ texture. In contrast, rocks made up of large grains have a

_____ texture.

19. How did the rock in Figure 8, on page 86, form?

_____

_____

_____

Review (p. 86)

Now that you've finished Section 1, review what you learned by answering the Review questions in your ScienceLog.

Section 2: Igneous Rock (p. 87)

1. What factors affect the type of igneous rock that forms from cooling magma? (Circle all that apply.)

   a. the composition of the magma
   b. the climate
   c. the amount of time it takes the magma to solidify
   d. the weather

Origins of Igneous Rock (p. 87)

2. How is the solidification of magma similar to water freezing?

_____

_____

_____

_____

_____

3. Under which of the following conditions can magma form? (Circle all that apply.)

   a. when rock is heated
   b. when pressure on rock is released
   c. when rock changes composition
   d. when rock is weathered by wind

Use Figure 9, on page 87, to answer the following questions.

4. All minerals have the same melting point. True or False? (Circle one.)

▲ ▲ CHAPTER 4

5. High pressure keeps minerals from melting deep within the Earth. True or False? (Circle one.)

6. How can the addition of fluids to a rock cause it to melt and form magma?

_____

_____

_____

Composition and Texture of Igneous Rock (p. 88)

7. Dark-colored rocks are usually _____ than light-colored rocks. (less dense or more dense)

8. Look at Figure 10 on page 88. Granite is probably _____ than gabbro. (less dense or more dense)

9. _____ igneous rocks are rich in elements such as silicon, sodium, and potassium. (Felsic or Mafic)

10. _____ igneous rocks are dark in color and contain iron, magnesium, and calcium. (Felsic or Mafic)

11. Look at Figure 11 on page 88. How does the cooling time of the magma affect the texture of the igneous rock that forms?

_____

_____

_____

_____

_____

Igneous Rock Formations (p. 89)

12. Intrusive rock usually has a coarse-grained texture. Why?

_____

_____

_____

13. Enchanted Rock, shown in Figure 12 on page 89, is a

   a. sill.
   c. laccolith.
   b. pluton.
   d. dike.

14. All of the following intrusive rock formations in Figure 13, on page 89, cut through existing land formations EXCEPT

   a. dikes.
   c. sills.
   b. batholiths.
   d. plutons.

15. Formations that are sandwiched between layers of existing

   rock formations are called _____ and

   _____ .

16. Look at the Brain Food on page 90. There is a type of igneous rock

   called _____ that can sometimes float.

17. Extrusive rock cools slowly. True or False? (Circle one.)

18. Extrusive igneous rock formations, such as lava flows, often

   _____ existing landforms.

Review (p. 90)

Now that you've finished Section 2, review what you learned by answering the Review questions in your ScienceLog.

Section 3: Sedimentary Rock (p. 91)

1. All of the following are causes of weathering EXCEPT

   a. sunlight.
   c. wind.
   b. water.
   d. air pressure.

Origins of Sedimentary Rock (p. 91)

2. How is natural cement formed?

_____

_____

_____

_____

3. Sedimentary rock forms near the Earth's core. True or False? (Circle one.)

4. Which of the following are good places to observe layers of sedimentary rock, or *strata*? (Circle all that apply.)

   a. road cuts
   c. in canyons carved by rivers
   b. construction zones
   d. flat plains

▲ ▲ **CHAPTER 4**

Chapter 4, continued

Composition of Sedimentary Rock (p. 92)

5. The three main categories of sedimentary rock are organic,

_____ and _____ .

6. What are clasts?

_____

_____

7. Look at Figure 17 on page 92. Breccia is made up of _____

fragments, while siltstone is made up of _____
fragments.

8. How does chemical sedimentary rock form?

_____

_____

_____

9. Chemical limestone forms
  a. on the ocean floor.
  b. within the Earth's mantle.
  c. in volcanoes.
  d. 16–25 km below the Earth's surface.

10. A type of rock called limestone can form from the remains of sea organisms. Explain.

_____

_____

_____

_____

_____

11. Most fossils come from land-dwelling organisms, such as

dinosaurs. True or False? (Circle one.)

Sedimentary Rock Structures (p. 94)

12. Stratification is the _____ of sediment.

13. The thickness of strata can be affected by the rate of

_____ of the sediment.

14. Look at Figure 21 on page 94. Cross-beds are

_____ deposits of sediment caused by the wind.

15. The ripple marks in the sedimentary rock in Figure 22, on page 94, were caused by

    a. the wind.   **c.** moving tectonic plates.

    b. a receding glacier.   **d.** flowing water.

Review (p. 94)

Now that you've finished Section 3, review what you learned by answering the Review questions in your ScienceLog.

Section 4: Metamorphic Rock (p. 95)

1. Metamorphic rock can form from other metamorphic rock.

True or False? (Circle one.)

Origins of Metamorphic Rock (p. 95)

2. A rock can undergo metamorphism when its

surroundings _____ .

3. At a depth of 16 km inside the Earth, the pressure is

_____ than the pressure at 2 km. (greater or less)

4. Why doesn't metamorphism occur at temperatures greater than about 1,000°C?

_____

_____

_____

5. Contact metamorphism occurs when rocks come in contact with

magma. True or False? (Circle one.)

6. How does regional metamorphism occur? (Circle all that apply.)

    a. Pressure builds up in rock that is deeply buried under other rock.

    b. Large pieces of the Earth's crust collide with each other.

    c. Rocks contact magma.

    d. Igneous intrusions "cook" the surrounding rock.

Composition of Metamorphic Rock (p. 97)

7. What happens to the minerals in rock when metamorphism occurs?

_____

_____

_____

_____

_____

8. Garnet, shown in Figure 26 on page 97, is formed when heat and

pressure cause the minerals _____ ,

_____ , and _____

to combine and recrystallize.

9. Look at Figure 27 on page 97. Suppose that a geologist finds the metamorphic mineral chlorite. At what depth did the mineral form?

a. 4–32 km   **c.** 5–34 km

b. 25–60 km   **d.** 30–70 km

Textures of Metamorphic Rock (p. 98)

10. A foliated rock has _____ grains.
(aligned or random)

11. What do all the rocks shown in Figure 28, on page 98, have in common?

_____

_____

12. Which of the following are nonfoliated metamorphic rocks?
(Circle all that apply.)

a. marble   **c.** quartzite

b. gneiss   **d.** sandstone

Review (p. 99)

Now that you've finished Section 4, review what you learned by answering the Review questions in your ScienceLog.

CHAPTER

5   DIRECTED READING WORKSHEET

Energy Resources

As you read Chapter 5, which begins on page 106 of your textbook, answer the following questions.

Imagine . . . (p. 106)

1. What are two advantages of solar cars over gasoline-powered cars?

_____

_____

2. Solar cars aren't an option for motorists because the technology isn't advanced enough. True or False? (Circle one.)

What Do You Think? (p. 107)

Answer these questions in your ScienceLog now. Then later, you'll have a chance to revise your answers based on what you've learned.

Investigate! (p. 107)

3. How will you compare the effectiveness of solar heating in the balloons in this activity?

_____

_____

Section 1: Natural Resources (p. 108)

4. Which of the following items does the atmosphere contribute to our "life support system" on Earth? (Circle all that apply.)

    a. shelter   **d.** rain
    b. food   **e.** air
    c. warmth   **f.** nutrients

5. Humans _____ their immediate surroundings by using natural resources. (change or adapt to)

6. Figure 1 shows products made from _____ .

_____

Chapter 5, continued

_____

Renewable Resources (p. 109)

7. Which of the following is an example of a renewable resource?

   a. trees

   b. oil

   c. natural gas

   d. coal

8. Many renewable resources are being used faster than they can be regenerated. True or False? (Circle one.)

Nonrenewable Resources (p. 109)

9. Why are resources such as natural gas and coal nonrenewable?

_____

_____

_____

_____

Conserving Natural Resources (p. 110)

10. Name one way you can help conserve a natural resource.

_____

_____

_____

_____

Review (p. 110)

Now that you've finished Section 1, review what you learned by answering the Review questions in your ScienceLog.

Section 2: Fossil Fuels (p. 111)

1. Fossil fuels are the _____ resources humans depend on most.

2. How is energy released from fossil fuels?

_____

_____

Chapter 5, continued

Liquid Fossil Fuels—Petroleum (p. 111)

Each of the following statements is false. Change the underlined word to make the statement true, and write the corrected statement in the space provided.

3. Liquid fossil fuels come from <u>petrification</u>.

_____

4. Crude oil is separated into fossil fuels and other products in <u>the Earth's crust</u>.

_____

_____

5. Some of the fossil fuels separated from petroleum are gasoline, diesel fuel, kerosene, and <u>corn oil</u>.

_____

_____

Gaseous Fossil Fuels—Natural Gas (p. 112)

6. Which of the following is NOT a component of natural gas?
   a. methane
   b. propane
   c. butane
   d. gasoline

Mark each of the following statements *True* or *False*.

7. _____ A vehicle fueled by natural gas produces more pollution than a vehicle fueled by gasoline.

8. _____ Natural gas is used for generating electricity.

Solid Fossil Fuels—Coal (p. 112)

9. How is coal different from the other fossil fuels?

_____

_____

10. One reason people use coal as an energy resource less today than in the early 1900s is because we now know that coal produces

large amounts of _____ .

CHAPTER 5

Chapter 5, continued

11. Coal is still burned by _____ to produce

_____ .

How Do Fossil Fuels Form? (p. 113)

12. Which fossil fuel(s) form from the remains of sea organisms?

_____

_____

13. Which fossil fuel(s) form from decayed swamp plants?

_____

_____

Choose the term in Column B that best matches the description in
Column A, and write the corresponding letter in the space provided.

Column A	Column B
____ **14.** stage of coal that is about 60 percent carbon	**a.** lignite
____ **15.** stage of coal that is about 70 percent carbon	**b.** anthracite
____ **16.** stage of coal that is about 80 percent carbon	**c.** peat
____ **17.** stage of coal that is about 90 percent carbon	**d.** bituminous coal

Review (p. 114)

Now that you've finished the first part of Section 2, review what you
learned by answering the Review questions in your ScienceLog.

Where Are Fossil Fuels Found? (p. 115)

18. Figure 9 shows regions in the United States where petroleum,
natural gas, and coal are found. List three states that have all
three fossil fuels.

_____

_____

_____

19. How much of the petroleum and petroleum products used in the United States is imported?

_____

_____

How Do Humans Obtain Fossil Fuels? (p. 115)

Mark each of the following statements *True* or *False*.

20. _____ To remove natural gas from the Earth, engineers drill wells into rock.

21. _____ Oil wells exist only on land.

22. _____ Strip mining is used to mine shallow coal deposits.

Problems with Fossil Fuels (p. 116)

23. Burning coal sometimes releases _____, which contributes to acid precipitation.

24. Describe two negative effects of acid precipitation.

_____

_____

25. Look at Figure 13. Why is working in a coal mine so dangerous?

_____

_____

_____

_____

26. Two problems associated with petroleum are

_____ and _____ .

Dealing with Fossil-Fuel Problems (p. 117)

27. How can you and your family help reduce the problems caused by fossil fuels?

_____

_____

_____

_____

CHAPTER 5

___

Chapter 5, continued

___

Review (p. 117)

Now that you've finished Section 2, review what you learned by answering the Review questions in your ScienceLog.

Section 3: Alternative Resources (p. 118)

1. Most electricity is produced from

    a. solar energy.   **c.** fossil fuels.

    b. hydroelectric power.   **d.** wind.

Splitting the Atom (p. 118)

Mark each of the following statements *True* or *False*.

2. _____ Most nuclear energy is produced by fission.

3. _____ Radioactive waste forms when nuclear energy is produced by fission.

4. Why might some people object to nuclear power plants?

_____

_____

_____

5. What is the purpose of the large tower in Figure 17?

_____

_____

_____

Combining Atoms (p. 119)

6. Fusion is safer than fission. Why isn't fusion used more often?

_____

_____

_____

_____

_____

_____

Chapter 5, continued

Sitting in the Sun (p. 119)

7. In the calculator in Figure 18, the light boxes at the top

are _____ , which are used to change

_____ into _____ .

8. A solar _____ collects solar energy
through thousands of solar cells.

9. Which of the following is NOT true about solar panels?

   a. They require little maintenance.
   b. They are relatively inexpensive to make.
   c. They produce no pollution when they are used.
   d. Many homes use them to produce electricity.

10. Look at Figure 21. Then arrange each of the following statements
in order to explain how a solar collector can give you a hot
shower by writing the appropriate number in the space provided.

   _____ Water is pumped to your shower.

   _____ Liquid moving through tubes increases in temperature.

   _____ Water is heated.

   _____ Sun shines into dark-colored boxes.

   _____ Liquid is pumped through tubes inside a water heater.

11. Large-scale solar power facilities use _____

to direct sunlight onto oil-filled _____ or

tanks filled with molten _____ .

12. *Solar Two* can generate enough energy to power 20,000 homes in
California. True or False? (Circle one.)

Capture the Wind (p. 122)

13. In the United States, most wind farms are found in

   a. Arizona.   **c.** New Mexico.
   b. Nevada.   **d.** California.

14. List three benefits of using wind power.

_____

_____

_____

_____

_____

CHAPTER 5

Chapter 5, continued

Review (p. 122)

Now that you've finished the first part of Section 3, review what you learned by answering the Review questions in your ScienceLog.

Hydroelectric Energy (p. 123)

15. How has the energy of falling water been used in the past?

_____

_____

_____

16. Hydroelectric energy is _____ produced

by _____ water.

17. Hydroelectric energy is renewable and is available everywhere. True or False? (Circle one.)

Powerful Plants (p. 124)

18. Energy resources consisting of plant parts and the dung of plant-grazing animals are called _____ .

19. Alcohol is made from _____ or

_____ that comes from plants.

20. A fuel made by combining gasoline with alcohol is called alcoline. True or False? (Circle one.)

Deep Heat (p. 125)

21. Energy that comes from deep within the Earth is called geyser energy. True or False? (Circle one.)

Review (p. 125)

Now that you've finished Section 3, review what you learned by answering the Review questions in your ScienceLog.

CHAPTER
6 **DIRECTED READING WORKSHEET**

The Rock and Fossil Record

As you read Chapter 6, which begins on page 132 of your textbook, answer the following questions.

What a Find! (p. 132)

1. Using only the skull and teeth of a dinosaur, what can you learn about the animal?

_____

_____

_____

What Do You Think? (p. 133)

Answer these questions in your ScienceLog now. Then later, you'll have a chance to revise your answers based on what you've learned.

Investigate! (p. 133)

2. What can scientists tell about an animal's diet by looking at its teeth?

_____

_____

_____

_____

_____

Section 1: Earth's Story and Those Who First Listened (p. 134)

3. Which of the following choices best describe the branch of Earth science called geology?

   a. the study of dinosaurs
   b. the study of Earth's history
   c. the study of herbivores
   d. the study of volcanoes

The Principle of Uniformitarianism (p. 134)

4. _____ outlined uniformitarianism, the main principle of modern geology.

Chapter 6, continued

5. The principle of uniformitarianism states that
    a. the Earth changed only at certain points throughout its history.
    b. the Earth changed more in its past than in its present.
    c. the same geologic processes shaping the Earth today have been at work throughout Earth's history.

6. What phrase summarizes uniformitarianism?

_____

_____

7. Number the following geologic processes in the correct sequence:

_____ Rivers carry rock particles downstream.

_____ In time, new rock will be uplifted and create new landforms.

_____ Rock particles are deposited and form new layers of sediment.

_____ Natural forces break down rock into smaller particles.

8. Why didn't other scientists immediately accept the theory of uniformitarianism?

_____

_____

_____

_____

9. The common belief concerning geologic change during Hutton's time was called _____.

10. The works of Charles Lyell, published from 1830 to 1833, were titled _____. These works successfully challenged the theory of _____.

Modern Geology—A Happy Medium (p. 136)

11. What present-day evidence suggests that the extinction of dinosaurs is the result of a catastrophic event?

_____

_____

_____

12. Modern geology is considered a _____ between catastrophism and uniformitarianism.

    a. happy medium   **c.** difference

    b. contrast   **d.** choice

Review (p. 136)

Now that you've finished Section 1, review what you learned by answering the Review questions in your ScienceLog.

Section 2: Relative Dating: Which Came First? (p. 137)

1. What clues do scientists use to study the Earth's history?

_____

_____

_____

2. Determining the age of objects or events in relation to other

objects or events is called _____.

The Principle of Superposition (p. 137)

3. As long as a sequence of rock layers is undisturbed, scientists

know that _____ rocks lie above

_____ rocks.

4. What phrase will help you remember the principle of superposition?

_____

_____

_____

The Geologic Column (p. 138)

5. How did geologists create the geologic column?

_____

_____

_____

_____

_____
Chapter 6, continued

Place each of the terms below in the correct order to complete the following sentence. Write the corresponding letter for each term in the appropriate blank.

6. Geologists will gather _____ about a _____ and

compare it with the _____ in order to determine the

sequence's _____ .

    a. age(s)   **c.** information

    b. geologic column(s)   **d.** rock sequence(s)

Disturbed Rock Layers (p. 139)

7. Why is a crosscutting feature always younger than the rock layers it cuts across?

_____

_____

_____

_____

Choose the term in Column B that best matches the description in Column A, and write your answer in the space provided.

Column A	Column B
____ **8.** a break in the Earth's crust along which blocks of crust slide relative to one another	**a.** superposition
____ **9.** younger sediment deposited on top of older layers	**b.** fold
____ **10.** molten rock that has squeezed into existing rock and hardened	**c.** fault
____ **11.** rock layers bent by the Earth's internal forces	**d.** tilt
____ **12.** rock layers slanted by the Earth's internal forces	**e.** intrusion

Gaps in the Record—Unconformities (p. 140)

13. When a layer or several layers of rock are missing from a rock-

layer sequence, the gaps are called unconformities. True or False? (Circle one.)

Chapter 6, continued

14. Name two possible explanations for a missing layer in a rock-layer sequence.

_____

15. From Figure 6, an unconformity is called

_____ if the missing layer was never actually present.

16. Nondeposition occurs when the supply of

_____ stops at some point and then

restart. _____ causes an unconformity when an area is exposed to water, wind, or other elements.

Types of Unconformities (p. 141)

Choose the term in Column B that best matches the description in Column A, and write your answer in the space provided. Terms may be used more than once.

Column A	Column B
____ **17.** found between horizontal layers and tilted layers	**a.** disconformity
____ **18.** where sedimentary rock layers lie on top of an eroded surface of nonlayered igneous or metamorphic rock	**b.** nonconformity
____ **19.** most common type of unconformity	**c.** angular unconformity
____ **20.** part of a sequence of parallel layers is missing	

Rock-Layer Puzzles (p. 141)

21. How do geologists figure out rock-layer puzzles?

_____

_____

_____

_____

Review (p. 141)

Now that you've finished Section 2, review what you learned by answering the Review questions in your ScienceLog.

Section 3: Absolute Dating: A Measure of Time (p. 142)

1. What is the purpose of absolute dating?

_____

_____

Radioactive Decay (p. 142)

2. Radioactive isotopes are used to determine the

_____ of rocks and fossils.

3. When an isotope is _____, it stays in its original form.
When an isotope is _____, it is called radioactive.
   a. unstable; stable
   b. stable; constant
   c. stable; unstable
   d. unstable; constant

4. How do scientists determine the age of an object using isotopes?

_____

_____

_____

_____

5. In Figure 10, a(n) _____ isotope is called
the parent material and, after radioactive decay, the

_____ isotope is called the daughter

material. (stable or unstable, stable or unstable)

Radiometric Dating (p. 143)

6. You can figure out the age of a rock sample if you know the

_____ for an element in the rock sample.

7. After every half-life, what has happened to the amount of parent
material present in an object?

_____

_____

_____

_____

Chapter 6, continued
_____

Types of Radiometric Dating (p. 144)

8. How do scientists know when people lived at Effigy Mounds?

_____

_____

_____

_____

_____

_____

Choose the radiometric dating method in Column B that best matches the description in Column A, and write your answer in the space provided. Terms may be used more than once.

Column A	Column B
_____ **9.** used to date rocks between 100,000 years and 10 million years old	**a.** uranium-lead
_____ **10.** used for dating objects less than 50,000 years old	**b.** potassium-argon
_____ **11.** used to date rocks older than 10 million years	**c.** carbon-14
_____ **12.** useful in dating plant and animal remains	
_____ **13.** parent material has a half-life of 4.5 billion years	

14. Carbon-12 is a stable isotope, while

_____ is a radioactive isotope.

15. The carbon-14 method of dating differs from the potassium-argon and the uranium-lead methods of dating by using

   a. the ratio of parent-to-daughter materials.
   b. ratios of carbon isotopes.
   c. more accurate technology.
   d. more unstable isotopes.

Review (p. 145)

Now that you've finished Section 3, review what you learned by answering the Review questions in your ScienceLog.

_____

Section 4: Looking at Fossils (p. 146)

1. What does studying fossils help you learn about Coralville?

_____

_____

_____

_____

_____

Fossilized Organisms (p. 146)

2. Fossils are formed in rocks when the _____
body parts of an organism get buried in

_____ and are preserved when it turns to

_____ .

Mark each of the following statements *True* or *False*.

3. _____ Fossils occur only when an organism dies and the remains are trapped between layers of rock.

4. _____ Some of our best insect fossils are preserved in hardened tree sap.

5. _____ One example of a fossil formed by mummification is petrified wood.

6. What are frozen fossils?

_____

_____

_____

_____

_____

7. The fossilized remains of some animals have been found in sticky

pools called _____ .

Other Types of Fossils (p. 148)

8. A _____ is naturally preserved evidence of
an animal's activity.

9. How do animal tracks and burrows become fossils?

_____

_____

_____

_____

_____

10. Coprolites are fossilized feces, which makes them a type of

_____ . (index fossil or trace fossil)

11. When sediment fills a mold and becomes rock, a

_____ is created.

Using Fossils to Interpret the Past (p. 149)

12. Which of the following can scientists interpret by examining fossils? (Circle all that apply.)

    a. how Earth's environment has changed over time

    b. how plants and animals have changed over time

    c. how rocks have changed positions

    d. the Earth's position relative to the Sun

13. What did the marine fossils discovered on top of Canadian mountaintops tell scientists?

    a. These marine species lived on top of prehistoric mountain-tops.

    b. Ancient humans must have moved these fossil remains.

    c. The rocks of the mountaintop were once below the surface of an ocean.

    d. The fossils were fake.

14. How do scientists know that fish existed before amphibians?

_____

_____

_____

_____

_____

_____

Using Fossils to Date Rocks (p. 150)

15. When geologists find an index fossil, what information do they know about the rock layer in which the fossil was found?

_____

_____

_____

_____

_____

16. Imagine that you were rock climbing and found a *Phacops* fossil. The rock surrounding this fossil is probably

_____ years old.

Review (p. 150)

Now that you've finished Section 4, review what you learned by answering the Review questions in your ScienceLog.

Section 5: Time Marches On (p. 151)

1. If you found a stack of photographs and wanted to make a model of a rock sequence, the _____ photographs would be placed on the top of the stack.

    a. oldest

    b. newest

    c. most accurate and highest resolution

    d. negative

2. Name two things scientists use to study the history of the Earth.

_____

_____

Rock Layers and Geologic Time (p. 151)

3. The layers of sedimentary rock exposed in the Grand Canyon show more of the geologic column than do most places on Earth.

The exposed layers represent nearly _____ years of geologic time.

The Geologic Time Scale (p. 152)

4. Why have geologists created the geologic time scale?

_____

_____

_____

_____

Using Figure 22, choose the name in Column B that best matches the eon described in Column A, and write your answer in the space provided.

Column A	Column B
_____ **5.** Earliest known rocks formed on Earth	**a.** Hadean eon
_____ **6.** Includes the present	**b.** Archean eon
_____ **7.** Moon rocks and meteorites found on Earth	**c.** Proterozoic eon
_____ **8.** First organisms with well-developed cells	**d.** Phanerozoic eon

Choose the geologic time division in Column B that best matches the description in Column A, and write your answer in the space provided.

Column A	Column B
_____ **9.** third largest division of geologic time	**a.** era
_____ **10.** second largest division of geologic time	**b.** period
_____ **11.** largest division of geologic time	**c.** epoch
_____ **12.** fourth largest division of geologic time	**d.** eon

13. All of the following are kinds of changes represented by the boundaries between geologic time intervals except

　a. the appearance or disappearance of life forms.
　b. changes in rock types.
　c. changes in global climate.
　d. changes in the Earth's position.

14. Life forms appeared on land during the beginning of the

　Paleozoic era. True or False? (Circle one.)

_____

Chapter 6, continued

_____

15. The Age of Reptiles is the _____ era.

16. Why is the Cenozoic era called the Age of Mammals?

_____

_____

_____

Can You Imagine 4.6 Billion Years? (p. 155)

17. Look at the Earth-history clock in Figure 26. How long did the Proterozoic Eon last according to that clock?

_____

_____

_____

18. According to the Earth-history clock in Figure 26, how long has the Cenozoic era lasted?

   a. 650 million years
   b. 1 hour
   c. 50,000 years
   d. 10 minutes

Review (p. 155)

Now that you've finished Section 5, review what you learned by answering the Review questions in your ScienceLog.

CHAPTER

7 **DIRECTED READING WORKSHEET**

Plate Tectonics

As you read Chapter 7, which begins on page 164 of your textbook, answer the following questions.

This Really Happened! (p. 164)

1. What have scientists learned from the GPS tracker on Mount Everest?

_____

_____

_____

2. What are some of the geologic events that are explained by plate tectonics?

_____

_____

_____

What Do You Think? (p. 165)

Answer these questions in your ScienceLog now. Then later, you'll have a chance to revise your answers based on what you've learned.

Investigate! (p. 165)

3. What will you do in this activity?

_____

_____

_____

_____

Section 1: Inside the Earth (p. 166)

4. Earth's layers of rock are classified by their

_____ and their

_____ .

CHAPTER 7

The Composition of the Earth (p. 166)

5. If you were to dig to the center of the Earth, in what order would you encounter the three major layers?

   a. core, mantle, crust
   b. mantle, crust, core
   c. crust, mantle, core
   d. crust, core, mantle

Choose the substance in Column B that best describes the composition of each Earth layer in Column A, and write the letter of the substance in the space provided.

Column A	Column B
_____ **6.** oceanic crust	**a.** granite
_____ **7.** continental crust	**b.** iron
_____ **8.** mantle	**c.** basalt
_____ **9.** core	**d.** iron and magnesium

10. Draw a circle graph showing the approximate percentages of Earth's mass in each layer. Use the circle given.

Earth's Mass

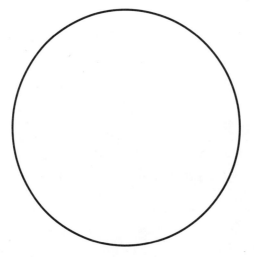

_____

Chapter 7, continued

_____

The Structure of the Earth (p. 168)

Complete the table.

	Physical layers of Earth	Physical properties	Thickness (in km)
11.		Rigid	15–300
12.		Solid rock that flows	
13.			2,550
14.	Outer core		
15.		Solid and dense	1,228

16. Tectonic plates are part of the _____ .

17. Look at the Biology Connection on page 169. Which of the following is included in the biosphere? (Circle all that apply.)

    a. the land surface
    b. the upper part of the mantle
    c. the lower part of the atmosphere
    d. the oceans

Tectonic Plates (p. 170)

18. Tectonic plates move around on top of the asthenosphere.

    True or False? (Circle one.)

19. Which of the following are characteristics of tectonic plates? (Circle all that apply.)

    a. They are sitting still.
    b. They are different sizes.
    c. Some are made of oceanic crust.
    d. Some are made of continental crust.

20. The South American tectonic plate only has continental crust.

    True or False? (Circle one.)

21. Why doesn't continental crust sink below the oceanic crust?

_____

_____

_____

_____

Mapping the Earth's Interior (p. 172)

22. _____ produce seismic waves.

23. No one has ever seen the inside of the Earth. How have scientists determined its internal structure?

_____

_____

_____

_____

_____

Review (p. 172)

Now that you've finished Section 1, review what you learned by answering the Review questions in your ScienceLog.

Section 2: Restless Continents (p. 173)

1. The coastlines of the continents South America and

_____ fit together like a jigsaw puzzle, as if they were joined sometime in the past. (North America or Africa)

Wegener's Theory of Continental Drift (p. 173)

2. Why is "continental drift" an appropriate title for Wegener's theory?

_____

_____

_____

3. Which of the following does the theory of continental drift explain? (Circle all that apply.)

a. the puzzle-like fit of the continents

b. fossils of the same species found on opposite sides of the Atlantic Ocean

c. the pattern of grooves left by glaciers

d. the reason ground water can be in short supply

The Breakup of Pangaea (p. 174)

4. Complete the diagram.

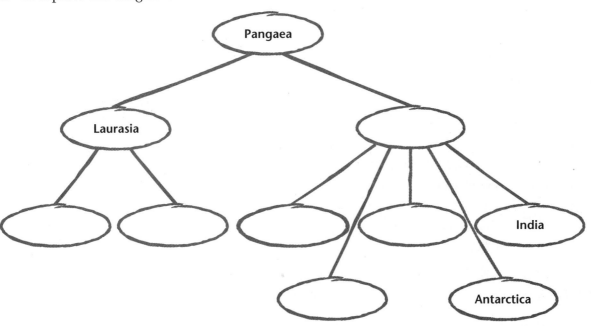

Sea-Floor Spreading (p. 175)

5. Explain why some scientists had difficulty accepting Wegener's theory of continental drift.

_____

_____

_____

6. What evidence supports the theory of continental drift?

_____

_____

_____

_____

_____

7. Some of the newest crust in the world forms along mid-ocean ridges. True or False? (Circle one.)

8. As the sea floor spreads, a gap is created that slowly grows wider as the continents drift apart. True or False? (Circle one.)

Magnetic Reversals (p. 176)

9. Compasses always point to the northern magnetic pole. If the Earth's magnetic field were reversed, a compass would point to

the _____ pole.

10. The magnetic minerals in rocks are permanently aligned with the Earth's magnetic field the moment the molten rock

_____ . (spreads or cools)

Review (p. 176)

Now that you've finished Section 2, review what you learned by answering the Review questions in your ScienceLog.

Section 3: The Theory of Plate Tectonics (p. 177)

1. The theory of plate tectonics replaced the theory of

_____ .

2. The theory of plate tectonics is that the Earth's

_____ is divided into plates that move

around on top of the _____ .

Possible Causes of Tectonic Plate Motion (p. 177)

3. Figure 13 of your text illustrates convection in the Earth's mantle. The diagram below illustrates convection in a pot of boiling water. Using the information given in Figure 13, explain why the water in the pot moves this way.

_____

_____

_____

4. For convection currents in the asthenosphere, where does the heat come from?

_____

_____

5. When oceanic plates slide down the slope of the lithosphere-asthenosphere boundary, the process is called

_____ . (ridge push or slab pull)

6. When gravity starts to pull tectonic plates into the asthenosphere, the process is called

_____ . (ridge push or slab pull)

Tectonic Plate Boundaries (p. 178)

7. At tectonic plate boundaries, tectonic plates separate,

_____ , or slide past each other.

Using Figure 14 as a reference, choose the type of plate boundary in Column B that best matches each description in Column A, and write the letter of the boundary in the space provided.

Column A	Column B
____ **8.** The Pacific plate is sliding past the North American plate along the San Andreas fault in the southwestern United States.	**a.** divergent boundaries **b.** transform boundaries
____ **9.** The Pacific plate is sliding under the South American plate, creating the Andes Mountains.	**c.** oceanic/oceanic collisions
____ **10.** The Indian plate is pushing into the Eurasian plate, creating the Himalayas.	**d.** continental/oceanic collisions
____ **11.** The African plate is moving away from the South American plate.	**e.** continental/continental collisions
____ **12.** The Pacific plate is sliding under the oceanic crust of Japan, forming an island area.	

13. When two plates collide and form a subduction zone as in Figure 14, an oceanic plate always sinks into the asthenosphere.

True or False? (Circle one.)

Tracking Tectonic Plate Motion (p. 180)

14. The device Wally Burg placed on Mount Everest is part of the GPS. How does the GPS help scientists track the movement of the mountain?

_____

_____

_____

_____

_____

Review (p. 180)

Now that you've finished Section 3, review what you learned by answering the Review questions in your ScienceLog.

Section 4: Deforming the Earth's Crust (p. 181)

1. Rocks may bend or break depending on how much

_____ is put on them.

Rocks Get Stressed (p. 181)

2. _____ is the type of stress that results

when plates collide, while _____ is the result of plates pulling away from each other.

Folding (p. 182)

3. Look at the second diagram of Figure 17. If a rock undergoes hori-

zontal stress, _____ and

_____ will form.

4. If both ends of a fold are still horizontal after folding, the fold is a

_____ .

Faulting (p. 183)

5. In Figure 19, a person is leaning against the

_____ , and another person is

suspended from the _____ .

6. In the diagram below, the hanging wall is on the

_____ . (left or right)

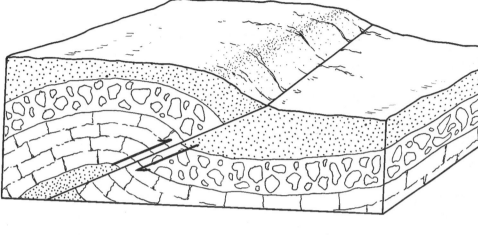

7. The diagram above shows a _____ fault.
(normal or reverse)

8. A _____ fault occurs when rocks break
and move horizontally due to opposing forces.
(reverse or strike-slip)

Plate Tectonics and Mountain Building (p. 185)

9. What is the reason that mountains exist?

_____

_____

_____

10. What are the three most common types of mountains?
   a. folded, dome, and volcanic
   b. folded, fault-block, and volcanic
   c. dome, fault-block, and volcanic
   d. folded, dome, and fault-block

11. Look at the Brain Food on page 185. Plate tectonics is responsible
for both the world's highest mountains and its deepest

_____ .

12. When the Appalachians first formed 390 million years ago, they
were located at the boundary between the North American and

African tectonic plates. True or False? (Circle one.)

Chapter 7, continued

Write the type of mountain illustrated in each diagram.

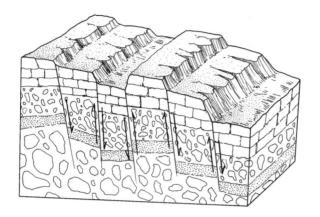

13. _____

14. _____

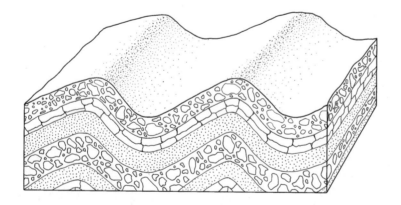

15. _____

Review (p. 187)

Now that you've finished Section 4, review what you learned by
answering the Review questions in your ScienceLog.

CHAPTER

8 | DIRECTED READING WORKSHEET

Earthquakes

As you read Chapter 8, which begins on page 194 of your textbook, answer the following questions.

Brace Yourself! (p. 194)

1. Where are you when the earthquake hits?

_____

_____

_____

2. Which of the following statements is NOT true of the Great Hanshin earthquake?

  a. It ruptured natural gas lines and broke water pipes.
  b. It lasted for two minutes.
  c. It left 300,000 people homeless.
  d. It destroyed almost 200,000 buildings.

3. According to the text, what will you study in this chapter?

_____

_____

_____

_____

What Do You Think? (p. 195)

Answer these questions in your ScienceLog now. Then later, you'll have a chance to revise your answers based on what you've learned.

Investigate! (p. 195)

4. What is the purpose of this activity?

_____

_____

_____

_____

_____

▲ CHAPTER 8

Chapter 8, continued

Section 1: What Are Earthquakes? (p. 196)

5. The science of studying earthquakes is called

_____ .

Where Do Earthquakes Occur? (p. 196)

For questions 6–8, determine whether each statement is true or false.
Then explain your answer.

6. Earthquakes happen only along tectonic plate boundaries.

_____

_____

_____

_____

7. Earthquakes only occur when plates push toward each other.

_____

_____

_____

_____

8. Look at Figure 1 at the bottom of page 196. The largest earthquake zone surrounds the Pacific Ocean.

_____

_____

_____

_____

What Causes Earthquakes? (p. 197)

9. If deformation is _____, it changes the
shape of rock, but does not cause earthquakes. If deformation is

_____ , it leads to earthquakes when the
stretched rock breaks and releases energy.

10. Elastic rebound occurs when rock suddenly returns to its
undeformed shape and causes an earthquake.

True or False? (Circle one.)

Are All Earthquakes the Same? (p. 198)

Use the chart and the diagram on pages 198 and 199 to answer the following questions.

11. _____ plate movement is associated with the strongest earthquakes. (Convergent or Divergent)

12. When an earthquake is caused by transform plate motion, the earthquake is likely to be moderate and shallow. True or False? (Circle one.)

13. Divergent motion creates _____ faults as blocks of _____ move away from each other. (reverse or normal, crust or mantle)

How Do Earthquakes Travel? (p. 200)

14. A _____ is a seismic wave that travels through the Earth's interior.

For statements 15–20, write a *P* in the space provided if the phrase is a characteristic of a P wave, and write an *S* in the space provided if the phrase is a characteristic of an S wave.

15. _____ This wave is also called a pressure wave.

16. _____ This wave is the slower of the two.

17. _____ This wave travels through solids, liquids, and gases.

18. _____ This wave is the fastest seismic wave.

19. _____ This wave shears rock back and forth.

20. _____ This wave travels only through solids.

21. If you experienced a surface wave, it might feel like you were riding on a roller coaster. True or False? (Circle one.)

22. Why are surface waves the most destructive waves?

_____

_____

_____

_____

Review (p. 201)

Now that you've finished Section 1, review what you learned by answering the Review questions in your ScienceLog.

▲▲ CHAPTER 8

Section 2: Earthquake Measurement (p. 202)

1. Seismologists want to find out which of the following things about an earthquake? (Circle all that apply.)

   a. when it started
   b. where it started
   c. how far it traveled
   d. how strong it was
   e. how much the ground moved

Locating Earthquakes (p. 202)

2. Seismographs create tracings of earthquake motion called

   _____ .

3. How do seismologists determine when an earthquake started?

   _____

   _____

   _____

   _____

4. The _____ of an earthquake is the place deep within the Earth where an earthquake begins. (epicenter or focus)

5. The _____ of an earthquake is on the surface of the Earth above where an earthquake begins. (epicenter or focus)

6. What is the name of the method seismologists use most to find the epicenter of an earthquake?

   a. the P-S method   c. the P-S time method
   b. the S-P method   d. the S-P time method

7. How do seismologists align the seismogram with the time-distance graph?

   _____

   _____

   _____

8. Refer to Figure 9 on page 203. Scientists figure out when an earthquake started by subtracting a wave's _____

   from the time when the wave was _____ .

9. Look at the diagram at the bottom of page 203. Once the seismologists know how far an epicenter is from a certain seismograph station, how do they find the location of the epicenter?

_____

_____

_____

_____

_____

_____

Measuring Earthquake Strength (p. 204)

10. Who is interested in the strength of earthquakes? (Circle all that apply.)

   a. seismologists   **c.** businesses

   b. public officials   **d.** safety organizations

11. On the modified Richter scale shown on page 204, an earthquake with a magnitude of _____ causes damage at the epicenter.

12. An earthquake with a magnitude of _____ would release 31.7 times as much energy as an earthquake with a magnitude of 6.0.

Review (p. 204)

Now that you've finished Section 2, review what you learned by answering the Review questions in your ScienceLog.

Section 3: Earthquakes and Society (p. 205)

1. Scientists have had no success in predicting earthquakes.

   True or False? (Circle one.)

Earthquake Hazard (p. 205)

2. What does a seismologist study to determine the earthquake-hazard level for a particular area?

_____

_____

_____

▲▲ **CHAPTER 8**

3. Look at Figure 10 at the bottom of page 205. Florida has a

_____ earthquake-hazard level.
(high or low)

Earthquake Forecasting (p. 206)

Mark each of the following statements *True* or *False*.

4. _____ It is difficult to predict when earthquakes will occur.

5. _____ The strength of earthquakes varies with how often
they occur.

6. _____ If an area has strong earthquakes, it never has
weaker earthquakes.

7. In your own words, explain how seismic gaps relate to the gap
hypothesis.

_____

_____

_____

Earthquakes and Buildings (p. 207)

8. Why do buildings sometimes collapse during an earthquake?

_____

_____

_____

9. Buildings can be designed to withstand the forces of an earthquake. True or False? (Circle one.)

Use the diagram on page 208 to answer the following questions.

10. Engineers design pipes with _____ that
help prevent water and gas lines from breaking.

11. A _____ is a large weight in a building's
roof that is shifted to counteract the building's movement.

12. _____ absorb seismic waves.

13. _____ are placed between floors to
counteract pressure put on the side of a building.

14. An _____ works like the weight in
question 11 but is located in the base of a building.

Are You Prepared for an Earthquake? (p. 209)

Read pages 209–210. Then answer the following questions.

15. Think of places you go during the day. What would you do if you were in one of these places when an earthquake happened?

_____

_____

_____

_____

_____

_____

Review (p. 210)

Now that you've finished Section 3, review what you learned by answering the Review questions in your ScienceLog.

Section 4: Earthquake Discoveries Near and Far (p. 211)

1. For what other research have scientists used seismic waves?

_____

_____

_____

Discoveries in Earth's Interior (p. 211)

2. By studying how seismic waves bend, scientists have learned a lot about Earth's interior. True or False? (Circle one.)

Use the diagram on page 211 to answer the following questions.

3. The shadow zone suggested that Earth has a solid core.

True or False? (Circle one.)

4. Which of the following describes the Moho?

   a. It marks the boundary between Earth's mantle and crust.
   b. It is an area where seismic waves slow down as they pass through it.
   c. It is an area where no seismic waves can be detected.
   d. It marks the area between Earth's mantle and inner core.

5. The Earth's inner core is _____ . (solid or liquid)

_____

Chapter 8, continued

_____

Quakes and Shakes on Other Cosmic Bodies (p. 212)

6. The first seismic testing on another cosmic body took place on

    a. Halley's comet.   **c.** the Moho.

    b. Mars.   **d.** the moon.

7. Explain the difference between seismic waves on Earth and those on the moon. What does this show?

_____

_____

_____

_____

_____

8. When *Viking 1* landed on Mars with a seismograph, the planet

was so _____ that the seismograph

worked mainly as a _____ .
(windy or cold, wind gauge or temperature gauge)

9. How do scientists measure seismic waves on the sun?

_____

_____

10. Seismic waves on the sun are caused by powerful magnetic disturbances in the sun. True or False? (Circle one.)

11. Sunquakes

    a. are weaker than earthquakes.
    b. last longer than earthquakes.
    c. are stronger than earthquakes.
    d. don't last as long as earthquakes.

Review (p. 213)

Now that you've finished Section 4, review what you learned by answering the Review questions in your ScienceLog.

CHAPTER

9 **DIRECTED READING WORKSHEET**

Volcanoes

As you read Chapter 9, which begins on page 220 of your textbook, answer the following questions.

This Really Happened! (p. 220)

1. Why was Auguste Ciparis hired by the Barnum & Bailey circus?

_____

_____

_____

_____

_____

What Do You Think? (p. 221)

Answer these questions in your ScienceLog now. Then later, you'll have a chance to revise your answers based on what you've learned.

Investigate! (p. 221)

2. What are you modelling in this activity?

_____

_____

_____

Section 1: Volcanic Eruptions (p. 222)

3. Volcanic eruptions can be _____ times stronger than the explosion produced by the first atomic bomb.

4. Most volcanic eruptions are _____ . (explosive or nonexplosive)

Nonexplosive Eruptions (p. 222)

5. All of the following can happen during nonexplosive eruptions EXCEPT

    a. lava flows.

    b. tons of rock are blasted into the air.

    c. lava forms fountains.

    d. rivers of red-hot lava form.

▲▲ CHAPTER 9

Explosive Eruptions (p. 223)

6. Which of the following would you expect to see during an explosive volcanic eruption? (Circle all that apply.)

    a. pieces of molten rock hardening in the air

    b. huge lava flows

    c. hot debris and gases moving at supersonic speeds

    d. a powerful explosion

7. A volcano must always grow in size after an eruption.

    True or False? (Circle one.)

8. Look at Figure 2 on page 223. When Mount St. Helens erupted in 1980, how many square kilometers of forest were damaged?

_____

_____

_____

Cross Section of a Volcano (p. 224)

Match each volcanic feature in Column B with the correct description in Column A, and write the corresponding letter in the appropriate space.

Column A	Column B
_____ **9.** hot liquid material below the Earth's surface	**a.** vent
_____ **10.** a combination of a vent and a buildup of lava or pyroclastic material on the Earth's surface	**b.** lava
_____ **11.** a hole or crack in the Earth's crust	**c.** magma
_____ **12.** molten material flowing on the Earth's surface	**d.** volcano

Magma (p. 224)

13. The more water contained in the magma, the

_____ the chances a violent eruption will

occur.

14. Silica-rich magma

    a. has a thin, runny consistency.

    b. allows gases to easily escape.

    c. causes explosive eruptions.

    d. is rarely associated with explosive volcanoes.

What Erupts from a Volcano? (p. 225)

15. _____ is the main product of a nonexplosive eruption, while the main product of an explosive eruption is _____ .

Use the descriptions and the photographs at the bottom of page 225 to mark each of the following statements *True* or *False*.

16. _____ Aa lava would be pleasant to walk across barefoot.

17. _____ Pahoehoe lava flows in a smooth sheet.

18. _____ Blocky lava moves quickly and spreads out evenly.

19. _____ Pillow lava's round shape is caused by contact with water.

20. When is pyroclastic material produced? (Circle all that apply.)

    a. as magma blasts from a volcano and solidifies in the air

    b. as lava flows solidify

    c. as existing rock is shattered by powerful explosions

    d. as eruptions cause earthquakes

Using the descriptions on page 226, match each type of pyroclastic material in Column B with the correct description in Column A, and write the corresponding letter in the appropriate space.

Column A	Column B
____ **21.** large blobs of magma that harden in the air	**a.** volcanic blocks
____ **22.** solid rock that is blasted out of a volcano	**b.** volcanic bombs
____ **23.** glasslike slivers from the walls of exploding gas bubbles	**c.** lapilli
____ **24.** pebble-like bits of magma that cool in the air	**d.** volcanic ash

▲▲ CHAPTER 9 ▲

25. Take a moment to look at the Biology Connection on page 226. Living near a volcano could be very dangerous. Why do so many people live close to volcanoes?

_____

_____

_____

_____

Review (p. 226)

Now that you've finished Section 1, review what you learned by answering the Review questions in your ScienceLog.

Section 2: Volcanoes' Effects on Earth (p. 227)

1. Volcanic eruptions have little effect on the Earth. True or False? (Circle one.)

An Explosive Impact (p. 227)

2. Figure 4 shows a cloud of volcanic ash flowing downhill. What might happen when an ash flow mixes with water?

_____

_____

_____

_____

3. Ash fallout can cause floods by damming up

_____ .

4. Place the following events in correct order to show how a single volcano can cause starvation and disease worldwide by writing the appropriate number in the space provided.

_____ Less sunlight reaches the Earth.

_____ There is a large-scale volcanic eruption.

_____ The Earth experiences longer, harsher winters and wetter, milder summers.

_____ The average global temperature drops.

_____ Worldwide food shortages occur because of widespread crop failures.

_____ Volcanic ash and sulfur-rich gases spread around the globe.

Different Types of Volcanoes (p. 228)

Match each volcano type in Column B with the correct description in Column A, and write the appropriate letter in the corresponding space. You may use the volcanoes in Column B more than once.

Column A	Column B
_____ **5.** the largest mountain on Earth	**a.** shield volcano
_____ **6.** forms from lava flows; not steep	**b.** cinder cone volcano
_____ **7.** often occurs in clusters	**c.** composite volcano
_____ **8.** forms from alternating layers of pyroclastic material and lava	
_____ **9.** made entirely of pyroclastic materials	

Craters and Calderas (p. 229)

10. The crater of a volcano is located in the magma chamber.

True or False? (Circle one.)

11. When the roof over an empty magma chamber collapses, it

forms a _____ . (crater or caldera)

Lava Plateaus (p. 229)

12. Which of the following are characteristics of a lava plateau? (Circle all that apply.)

  a. It is made of runny lava that solidifies.
  b. It comes from a single volcano.
  c. It may cover thousands of square kilometers.
  d. It is the result of a nonexplosive eruption.

Review (p. 229)

Now that you've finished Section 2, review what you learned by answering the Review questions in your ScienceLog.

Section 3: What Causes Volcanoes? (p. 230)

1. To help predict eruptions, scientists often rely on

_____ based on rock samples.

Chapter 9, continued

The Formation of Magma (p. 230)

2. Volcanoes begin to form in the deeper regions of the

_____ and the uppermost layers of the

_____ , in pockets where magma collects.

3. The rock of the Earth's mantle is NOT

   a. liquid.   **c.** hot.

   b. pliable.   **d.** under pressure.

4. Rock usually melts to form magma

   a. when there is an increase in pressure.

   b. when there is a decrease in pressure.

   c. when there is a decrease in temperature.

   d. when it is in a volcano.

5. How does magma behave like air bubbles that form on the bottom of a pan of boiling water?

_____

_____

_____

_____

_____

6. Magma is often a mixture of liquid and solid mineral crystals.

True or False? (Circle one.)

Where Volcanoes Form (p. 231)

7. Why are the plate boundaries surrounding the Pacific Ocean called the *Ring of Fire*?

_____

_____

_____

8. When two tectonic plates separate, a rift forms between the plates at the divergent boundary. True or False? (Circle one.)

9. Use the text on page 232 and Figure 10 to place the following steps of mid-ocean ridge formation in the correct order by writing the appropriate number in the space provided.

_____ Magma rises to the surface of the surrounding rock.

_____ Mantle material rises to fill the space between plates.

_____ New crust on the ocean floor is formed by the magma.

_____ A rift forms as tectonic plates move apart.

_____ The mantle rock melts because of the decrease in pressure.

10. _____ is the movement of one plate under another. (Subduction or Subversion)

11. The oceanic crust is _____ and _____ than the continental crust.

12. Convergent boundaries commonly occur where continental crust is subducted under oceanic crust. True or False? (Circle one.)

13. As the ocean crust sinks deeper into the mantle

    a. it increases in temperature.   **c.** it forms a volcano.

    b. it forms a lava fountain.   **d.** its pressure decreases.

Hot Spots (p. 233)

14. The Hawaiian Islands are located along a boundary between tectonic plates. True or False? (Circle one.)

15. Hot spots are above mantle plumes, which are columns of rising

_____ .

16. How could the same hot spot have formed all of the Hawaiian Islands?

_____

_____

_____

_____

_____

_____

_____

▲▲ **CHAPTER 9**
▲

_____

Chapter 9, continued

_____

Predicting Volcanic Eruptions (p. 234)

17. _____ volcanoes have erupted in
recorded history but are not erupting now. (Dormant or Extinct)

18. Active volcanoes include only those volcanoes currently

erupting. True or False? (Circle one.)

19. Just before an eruption, the number and intensity of small earth-

quakes _____ . (increase or decrease)

20. What might cause a bulge in the slope of a volcano?

_____

_____

_____

21. Answer this question after you finish reading pages 234 and 235.
Which of the following do scientists use to help predict volcanic
explosions? (Circle all that apply.)

    a. seismographs
    b. changes in a volcano's ultraviolet radiation
    c. the ratio of volcanic gases escaping from a volcano
    d. tiltmeters
    e. the angle of a volcano's slope
    f. changes in a volcano's surface temperature
    g. satellite images
    h. the frequency of earthquakes near a volcano
    i. scanning tunneling microscopes

Review (p. 235)

Now that you've finished Section 3, review what you learned by
answering the Review questions in your ScienceLog.

CHAPTER

10 DIRECTED READING WORKSHEET

Weathering and Soil Formation

As you read Chapter 10, which begins on page 244 of your textbook, answer the following questions.

How Do They Do That? (p. 244)

1. Why are river rocks round?

_____

_____

_____

_____

2. The words on the rocks that are pictured on this page were cut by

   a. water.   **c.** a laser.

   b. sand.   **d.** a chisel.

What Do You Think? (p. 245)

Answer these questions in your ScienceLog now. Then later, you'll have a chance to revise your answers based on what you've learned.

Investigate! (p. 245)

3. This activity looks at how weathering affects

   _____ and _____,

   which are two types of rock.

Section 1: Weathering (p. 246)

4. Rocks on the Earth's surface are constantly being broken down

   into smaller pieces. True or False? (Circle one.)

5. The breakdown of rock into smaller and smaller pieces can occur

   by _____ and _____

   means.

Mechanical Weathering (p. 246)

Mark each of the following questions *True* or *False*.

6. _____ Physical processes cause mechanical weathering.

7. _____ Ice, wind, gravity, and plants are all agents of
   mechanical weathering.

Chapter 10, continued

8. Look at the Chemistry Connection on page 246. When water freezes, it

    a. becomes more dense.

    b. decreases in volume.

    c. becomes a gas.

    d. expands.

9. What caused the granite shown in Figure 1 to break apart?

_____

_____

_____

_____

_____

_____

10. Gravity, water, and wind can all cause rocks to grind against

each other, which wears away exposed surfaces. True or False? (Circle one.)

11. Which of the following are examples of abrasion? (Circle all that apply.)

    a. one rock falling against another rock

    b. wind blowing sand against rock

    c. pebbles bumping against each other in a stream

    d. sunlight striking a rock

12. Figure 3 shows a ventifact, a rock that has been shaped by

_____ .

13. Can a plant break a rock apart? Explain.

_____

_____

_____

_____

_____

14. Animals that _____ , such as earthworms

and ants, cause _____ weathering.

Chapter 10, continued

Chemical Weathering (p. 249)

Mark each of the following questions *True* or *False*.

15. _____ Chemical weathering changes rocks into new substances.

16. _____ Figure 7 shows that granite will eventually turn into sand and clay due to chemical weathering.

17. _____ Over time, granite will dissolve in water.

18. _____ Nitric and sulfuric acid occur naturally in rain.

19. _____ The statue shown in Figure 8 was weathered by normal precipitation.

20. _____ The gases produced by burning fossil fuels can combine with water to form acid precipitation.

21. What does the cave shown in Figure 9 have to do with chemical weathering?

_____

_____

_____

22. Which of the following statements are true of lichens? (Circle all that apply.)

a. They contribute to mechanical weathering.
b. They make organic acids.
c. They live only in mild climates.
d. They are an alga and a fungus living together.

23. What caused the rust on the car in Figure 11?

_____

_____

_____

24. According to Figure 12, why is the rock at Capitol Reef National Park red?

_____

_____

Review (p. 251)

Now that you've finished Section 1, review what you learned by answering the Review questions in your ScienceLog.

CHAPTER 10

Section 2: Rates of Weathering (p. 252)

1. The rate at which a rock weathers can be affected by

_____ and _____ ,

as well as what the rock is made of.

Differential Weathering (p. 252)

2. Why does granite usually weather much slower than limestone?

_____

_____

_____

_____

_____

3. Devil's Tower, which was shaped by differential weathering, was once

    a. the core of a volcano.   **c.** a lava flow.
    b. a lava tube.   **d.** a coral reef.

The Shape of Weathering (p. 253)

4. Which weather faster: small rocks or large rocks? Why?

_____

_____

_____

_____

_____

_____

Weathering and Climate (p. 254)

5. Oxidation happens quickest in climates that are

_____ and _____ .

6. Chemical weathering affects rocks more in a temperate climate

than in a desert climate. True or False? (Circle one.)

Chapter 10, continued

Weathering and Elevation (p. 254)

7. Why would rocks at the top of a mountain weather faster than rocks at the base of a mountain?

_____

_____

_____

Review (p. 254)

Now that you've finished Section 2, review what you learned by answering the Review questions in your ScienceLog.

Section 3: From Bedrock to Soil (p. 255)

1. Soil contains _____ fragments and

_____ material.

Sources of Soil (p. 255)

Choose the term in Column B that best matches the description in Column A, and write your answer in the space provided.

Column A	Column B
_____ **2.** is moved by wind or water from one place to another	**a.** parent rock
_____ **3.** is formed from the bedrock below it	**b.** residual soil
_____ **4.** is the source of soil	**c.** transported soil
_____ **5.** is formed from decayed plants and animals	**d.** humus

Soil Layers (p.256)

Use Figure 18 and the text on page 256 to mark the following questions *True* or *False*.

6. _____ Soil often ends up in a series of horizontal layers.

7. _____ Topsoil can take hundreds of years to form.

8. _____ Topsoil is another name for Horizon C.

9. _____ Leaching occurs as substances dissolved from bedrock move up through layers of soil.

10. _____ Clays are found in the subsoil.

11. Under Horizon C is _____ .

Soil and Climate (p. 257)

12. The development of soil is affected by climate. True or False? (Circle one.)

13. Why is tropical topsoil thin?

_____

_____

_____

_____

14. Because of the sun and wind, deserts have a very high rate of chemical weathering. True or False? (Circle one.)

15. When ground water evaporates in the desert, it can leave behind _____ that can cause the soil to become _____ to plants.

16. What is so special about soil formation in the "breadbasket" of the United States?

_____

_____

_____

_____

_____

_____

17. Soils in arctic climates are
  a. similar to soils in tropical climates.
  b. similar to soils in desert climates.
  c. similar to soils in temperate climates.
  d. very different from soils in other climates.

Review (p. 258)

Now that you've finished Section 3, review what you learned by answering the Review questions in your ScienceLog.

Section 4: Soil Conservation (p. 259)

1. The ways _____ take care of the soil is
called soil conservation.

The Importance of Soil (p. 259)

2. Why do the plants shown in Figure 23 look so different from one
another?

_____

_____

_____

_____

_____

_____

_____

_____

_____

3. Which of the following statements are true of prairie dogs?
(Circle all that apply.)

   a. They live in trees.

   b. They live in soil.

   c. Soil is a large part of their diet.

   d. They help make humus.

4. Without soil, water would quickly flow to the ocean when it rains.

   True or False? (Circle one.)

Preventing Soil Erosion (p. 260)

5. Plants need soil to grow, but why does soil need plants?

_____

_____

_____

_____

_____

CHAPTER 10

6. After a harvest, a farmer might plant a cover crop to replace

_____ in the soil and prevent soil

_____ .

7. Crop rotation helps prevent

    a. overuse of pesticides.
    b. soil erosion due to wind.
    c. loss of nutrients in the soil.
    d. soil erosion due to water.

8. What do terracing and contour plowing have in common?

_____

_____

_____

_____

_____

_____

_____

9. Suppose you are a farmer who owns a field in a mountainous area.
Would you use contour plowing or terracing on your field?
Explain.

_____

_____

_____

_____

_____

_____

_____

Review (p. 261)

Now that you've finished Section 4, review what you learned by
answering the Review questions in your ScienceLog.

CHAPTER
11 DIRECTED READING WORKSHEET

The Flow of Fresh Water

As you read Chapter 11, which begins on page 268 of your textbook, answer the following questions.

Imagine . . . (p. 268)

1. What do you think caused the river to change so suddenly?

_____

_____

_____

_____

2. What topics will be covered in this chapter?

_____

_____

_____

_____

What Do You Think? (p. 269)

Answer these questions in your ScienceLog now. Then later, you'll have a chance to revise your answers based on what you've learned.

Investigate! (p. 269)

3. This exercise models how water flows underground. True or False? (Circle one.)

Section 1: The Active River (p. 270)

4. What process formed the Grand Canyon?

_____

_____

_____

_____

Chapter 11, continued

Water, Water Everywhere (p. 270)

When you finish reading page 271, choose the term in Column B that best matches the phase of the water cycle in Column A, and write the corresponding letter in the appropriate space.

Column A	Column B
____ **5.** Liquid water on Earth's surface changes into water vapor in the air.	**a.** precipitation
____ **6.** Water vapor in the air changes into liquid droplets, forming clouds.	**b.** percolation
____ **7.** Water falls from clouds onto the Earth's surface.	**c.** runoff
____ **8.** Water on land seeps into the ground.	**d.** infiltration
____ **9.** Water flows across the ground and collects in rivers or streams.	**e.** evaporation
____ **10.** Water in the ground moves downward through spaces in the soil.	**f.** condensation

River Systems (p. 272)

11. River systems are formed by networks of rivers and streams called

tributaries. True or False? (Circle one.)

12. Drainage basins are also called _____ .

13. What is the largest drainage basin in the United States?

_____

_____

14. Look at Figure 2. The Continental Divide runs along the
  a. Mississippi River.
  b. Missouri River.
  c. Rocky Mountains.
  d. Gulf of Mexico.

Stream Erosion (p. 273)

15. How is a river's channel formed?

_____

_____

_____

16. A stream with a high gradient is probably on a

_____ , and its water flows rapidly and has

_____ erosive energy.

17. List two things that would cause a stream's discharge to increase.

_____

_____

18. A fast river can carry _____ particles than a slow river. (larger or smaller)

19. Look at the illustrations on page 274. A river looks muddy

because of its _____ load.

The Stages of a River (p. 275)

20. Do all rivers erode at the same rate? Why or why not?

_____

_____

_____

21. A mature river flows faster than a youthful river.

True or False? (Circle one.)

Choose the type of river in Column B that best matches the description in Column A, and write the corresponding letter in the appropriate space. River types may be used more than once.

Column A	Column B
____ **22.** good drainage and high discharge	**a.** youthful river
____ **23.** flood plains	**b.** mature river
____ **24.** waterfalls and rapids	**c.** old river
____ **25.** steplike terraces	**d.** rejuvenated river
____ **26.** erodes its channel wider, not deeper	
____ **27.** extremely low erosive power	

Review (p. 276)

Now that you've finished Section 1, review what you learned by answering the Review questions in your ScienceLog.

Section 2: Stream and River Deposits (p. 277)

1. Deposition destroys productive soil. True or False? (Circle one.)

Deposition in Water (p. 277)

2. Deposition occurs in locations where a stream

_____ , such as where it enters a

_____ . (slows down or speeds up,
lake or waterfall)

3. If you were a miner in California, where would you choose to pan
for gold?

_____

_____

_____

_____

4. A river can cause a coastline to grow when a

_____ forms.

Deposition on Land (p. 279)

5. Alluvial fans are usually found

   a. at the top of a mountain.
   b. along the side of a mountain.
   c. at the base of a mountain.

6. Suppose you want to buy a farm. Name an advantage and a
disadvantage to choosing a farm that is located in a flood plain.

_____

_____

_____

_____

Review (p. 279)

Now that you've finished Section 2, review what you learned by
answering the Review questions in your ScienceLog.

Section 3: Water Underground (p. 280)

1. What is ground water?

_____

_____

_____

Location of Ground Water (p. 280)

2. The spaces between the rock and soil particles in the zone of

_____ are filled with water only when it

rains, but in the zone of _____ the spaces
are always filled with water.

3. What causes the water table to change?

_____

_____

_____

Aquifers (p. 280)

4. A rock layer must be _____ and

_____ in order to be considered
an aquifer.

Mark each of the following statements *True* or *False*.

5. _____ A rock is permeable if it stops the flow of water.

6. _____ Aquifers are often formed from sandstone.

7. _____ Some cities obtain their water supply from aquifers.

8. _____ Aquifers release water into recharge zones.

9. _____ A recharge zone is a location in an aquifer where
water is removed for agriculture.

Springs and Wells (p. 281)

10. Ground water moves toward _____
elevations.

11. Lakes form in areas where the water table is

_____ the Earth's surface.

12. An artesian formation consists of a sloping aquifer between

layers of _____ rock.

13. The pressurized water of an artesian spring flows through cracks

in the _____ .

14. A well can provide water as long as the bottom of the well stays

below the level of the _____ .

Underground Erosion and Deposition (p. 283)

Answer the following questions after reading pages 283–284. Choose
the term in Column B that best matches the phrase in Column A,
and write the corresponding letter in the appropriate space.

Column A	Column B
____ **15.** a type of limestone deposited by water	**a.** stalagmite
____ **16.** icicle-shaped feature that forms on the roof of a cave	**b.** stalactite
____ **17.** cone-shaped feature that forms on the floor of a cave	**c.** dripstone
____ **18.** circular depression formed by a collapsing cave	**d.** sinkhole

Review (p. 284)

Now that you've finished Section 3, review what you learned by
answering the Review questions in your ScienceLog.

Section 4: Using Water Wisely (p. 285)

1. Why is it important to use water wisely? (Circle all that apply.)

    a. Only a small amount of Earth's water is drinkable.

    b. Most of Earth's drinkable water is frozen.

    c. All living things need water.

    d. Water is a liquid.

Water Pollution (p. 285)

2. _____ -source pollution is easier to

control than _____ -source pollution.
(Point or Nonpoint, point or nonpoint)

After reading page 285, label each of the following sources of pollution with a *P* for point-source or an *NP* for nonpoint-source.

3. _____ street gutters

4. _____ factory drains

5. _____ fertilizers

6. _____ salts from irrigation

7. _____ acid rain

8. _____ eroded soils and silt from farming and logging

9. _____ drainage from mines

10. _____ sewer pipes

11. Farm irrigation like that in Figure 20 is a type of nonpoint-source pollution. True or False? (Circle one.)

Cleaning Polluted Water (p. 286)

12. Sewage treatment plants help prevent the spread of disease.

True or False? (Circle one.)

Place the following processing steps at a sewage treatment plant in order by placing the appropriate number in the corresponding space.

13. _____ Chlorine is added to disinfect the water.

14. _____ The water is mixed with oxygen and bacteria.

15. _____ Oil and scum are skimmed off the surface.

16. _____ Small particles sink and are filtered out.

17. _____ Water is released into a stream, lake, or ocean.

18. _____ Materials such as paper and bottle caps are caught by a screen.

19. _____ Bacteria eat the wastes and use the oxygen.

20. _____ Secondary treatment begins.

21. After waste water has been treated with the bacteria in the bottom of a septic tank, it flows into a

_____ , a set of buried pipes that distributes the water into the ground.

Where the Water Goes (p. 287)

22. Figure 23 shows that an average household in the United States uses most of its water for drinking and cooking.

True or False? (Circle one.)

Chapter 11, continued

---

23. Industries can conserve water by _____ it in their production processes.

24. In the United States, water used in factories is usually never recycled. True or False? (Circle one.)

25. Why can ground water be considered both a renewable and a nonrenewable resource?

_____

_____

_____

_____

_____

_____

_____

26. According to the Brain Food on page 289, the Ogallala aquifer is being used 10 times faster than it is refilling. True or False? (Circle one.)

27. The Ogallala aquifer is used most heavily for

   a. farming.   **c.** hydroelectric plants.
   b. drinking water.   **d.** swimming.

28. How are water resources different from other resources?

   a. Water levels cannot be monitored.
   b. There is no alternative resource that fulfills water's role in maintaining life.
   c. It is impossible to protect water resources.

Review (p. 289)

Now that you've finished Section 4, review what you learned by answering the Review questions in your ScienceLog.

CHAPTER

12 **DIRECTED READING WORKSHEET**

Agents of Erosion and Deposition

As you read Chapter 12, which begins on page 296 of your textbook, answer the following questions.

This Really Happened! (p. 296)

1. In 1998, a landslide in Malibu, California, caused several houses to fall into the ocean. How did waves start the landslide?

_____

_____

_____

_____

2. What will you study in this chapter? (Circle all that apply.)

a. the force of waves on coastlines
b. the best way to build a house on the coast
c. how the landscape is affected by gravity and moving ice
d. how the force of waves changes the landscape

What Do You Think? (p. 297)

Answer these questions in your ScienceLog now. Then later, you'll have a chance to revise your answers based on what you've learned.

Investigate! (p. 297)

3. What is the purpose of this activity?

_____

_____

Section 1: Shoreline Erosion and Deposition (p. 298)

4. A body of water meets land at a place called a

_____ .

Wave Energy (p. 298)

5. What do the ripples on the ocean have in common with the ripples that are produced when you blow on a cup of hot chocolate?

_____

Chapter 12, continued

Mark each of the following statements *True* or *False*.

6. _____ The strength of the wind and the length of time the wind blows affect the size of the wave.

7. _____ The surfer in California, shown in Figure 1, could be riding a wave produced by a storm near Australia.

8. _____ Waves travel alone.

9. Place the following steps in the correct sequence for the formation of breaking waves, or surf, by writing the corresponding number in the appropriate space.

_____ The top of a wave becomes too tall to support itself.

_____ Taller, more closely spaced waves are produced.

_____ The ocean floor crowds the bottom of the wave.

_____ The wave begins to curl and break.

_____ A wave train approaches the shore, and the waves change form.

_____ Waves travel away from their source in wave trains.

10. Waves break at regular intervals because they travel in

_____ .

11. The time interval between breaking waves is called the

_____ and usually lasts 10–20 seconds.

12. Waves are effective at moving material because they release a lot of energy when they break. True or False? (Circle one.)

13. Which of the following is NOT true of crashing waves?
   a. They produce solid rock.   **c.** They form beaches.
   b. They polish sand.   **d.** They throw rocks.

Wave Deposits (p. 300)

14. Any area of the shoreline made up of wave-deposited material is a beach. True or False? (Circle one.)

15. Beach materials come only from coastal areas. True or False? (Circle one.)

16. How do the pictures in Figure 4 show that not all beaches are the same? Give an example.

_____

_____

_____

_____

_____

_____

_____

17. The most common beach material is light-colored

_____ .

18. Where can you find a beach made of pebbles and larger rocks?

    a. Florida   **c.** tropical islands

    b. Hawaii   **d.** areas with stormy seas

19. A movement of water _____ to and near the shoreline is called a longshore current. (perpendicular or parallel)

20. Which of the following landforms are created by deposits due to longshore currents? (Circle all that apply.)

    a. a sea cliff   **c.** a barrier spit

    b. a sandbar   **d.** a bay

Wave Erosion (p. 301)

21. What two factors determine how quickly sea cliffs erode?

_____

_____

_____

_____

_____

Take a few moments to look over pages 302–303. Choose the term in Column B that best matches the description in Column A, and write the corresponding letter in the space provided.

Column A	Column B
_____ **22.** surrounding rock erodes, leaving a cliff that protrudes from the shoreline	**a.** sea cave
_____ **23.** wave action erodes a sea cave until it completely cuts through the rock	**b.** wave-cut terrace
_____ **24.** level platform beneath the water	**c.** sea stack
_____ **25.** isolated columns of rock that were once part of the mainland	**d.** headland
_____ **26.** large holes in rock along the base of cliffs	**e.** sea arch

Review (p. 303)

Now that you've finished Section 1, review what you learned by answering the Review questions in your ScienceLog.

Section 2: Wind Erosion and Deposition (p. 304)

1. How do plants reduce wind erosion?

_____

_____

_____

Process of Wind Erosion (p. 304)

2. When the wind causes sand-sized particles to bounce and skip along, the movement is called sedimentation.

True or False? (Circle one.)

3. The area of the Painted Desert, pictured in Figure 9 on page 305, shows the results of abrasion. True or False? (Circle one.)

4. What is the name for depressions in the sand that can be hundreds of meters wide and many meters deep?

_____

5. Nature's way of sandblasting rock with strong wind and loose

sand is called _____ .

Chapter 12, continued

Wind-Deposited Materials (p. 306)

6. When the wind blows _____, it can pick up and carry more material. Heavier material is deposited first

when the wind _____ .
(fast or slow, speeds up or slows down)

7. Place the following in the correct sequence for the formation of sand dunes by writing the appropriate number in the space provided.

_____ Collecting material creates an additional obstacle.

_____ Wind deposits more material, forming a mound or dune.

_____ Slowing wind drops the heavier particles.

_____ Wind hits a rock, plant, or other object and slows down.

_____ The original object eventually becomes buried.

8. Which of the following is NOT true of sand dunes?

a. They migrate in the direction of the wind.
b. Material is constantly transported up the slip face of the dune.
c. Different wind conditions produce differently shaped dunes.
d. Sand moves over the crest and slides down the steeply sloped side of the dune.

9. Take a moment to read "Disappearing Dunes and the Desert Tortoise" at the bottom of page 307. How are dune buggies endangering the desert tortoise's habitat?

_____

_____

_____

10. The fine-grained, windblown sediment called loess feels a lot like

_____ powder.

Each of the following statements is false. Change the underlined word to make the statement true, and write the correct word in the space provided.

11. Loess deposits are sometimes found far away from their source, because wind can carry <u>coarse-grained</u> material long distances.

_____

12. Many loess deposits came from glacial deposits during the last <u>global warming</u>.

_____

▲ ▲ **CHAPTER 12**
▲

13. Loess deposits are responsible for the destruction of many of the grain-growing areas of the world. True or False? (Circle one.)

14. Take a look at the Biology Connection in the left column of page 308. How did the sidewinder get its name?

_____

_____

_____

Review (p. 308)

Now that you've finished Section 2, review what you learned by answering the Review questions in your ScienceLog.

Section 3: Erosion and Deposition by Ice (p. 309)

1. How are a glacier and a sliding ice cube similar?

_____

_____

Glaciers—Rivers of Ice (p. 309)

2. Areas where glaciers form are so cold that you can chill a can of juice just by carrying it outside. True or False? (Circle one.)

3. Glaciers are found in _____ regions and

areas at _____ elevations.

4. Place the following in the correct sequence for the formation of glaciers by writing the appropriate number in the space provided.

_____ Gravity pulls on the gigantic mass of the ice packs, setting them in motion.

_____ Snow piles up year after year.

_____ A huge mass of ice is formed.

_____ The weight of the uppermost layers of snow causes the deep-packed snow to become ice crystals.

5. Alpine and oceanic are the two main types of glaciers.

True or False? (Circle one.)

6. Which of the following is NOT true of valley-type alpine glaciers?

    a. They flow slowly downhill, widening and straightening valleys.

    b. They form in valleys created by stream erosion.

    c. They form in mountainous areas.

    d. They spread across entire continents.

7. A continental ice sheet is the largest type of continental glacier.

    True or False? (Circle one.)

8. How large is the ice sheet that covers Antarctica?

_____

_____

_____

9. The largest ice shelf covers an area of ocean about the size of Texas. What is the name of this ice shelf?

_____

10. What makes an iceberg so hazardous to ships?

    a. Most of the iceberg cannot be seen above the water.

    b. An iceberg can suddenly "pop up" without warning.

    c. Huge pieces of falling ice can crush ships.

Mark each of the following statements *True* or *False*.

11. _____ A thick glacier moves faster than a thin glacier.

12. _____ Some glaciers move when the ice on the bottom starts to melt from the weight of the ice on top.

13. _____ The rate at which a glacier moves is the same throughout the glacier.

14. _____ The surface of a glacier flows more slowly than the glacier's base.

15. Look at Figure 16 on page 311. Why is the crevasse a hazard to the mountain climbers?

_____

_____

_____

_____

▲ ▲ **CHAPTER 12**

Chapter 12, continued

Landforms Carved by Glaciers (p. 312)

Complete the following questions after reading pages 312–314.

16. Rugged landforms are carved out by _____
glaciers. (alpine or continental)

17. Smooth and flattened landscapes are formed by

_____ glaciers. (alpine or continental)

Choose the term in Column B that best matches the description in
Column A, and write the corresponding letter in the space provided.

Column A	Column B
_____ **18.** carved by smaller glaciers that join the main glacier	**a.** horns
_____ **19.** glacial ice cuts into mountain walls and forms these bowl-like depressions	**b.** hanging valleys
_____ **20.** pyramid-shaped peaks formed by three or more depressions	**c.** arêtes
_____ **21.** jagged ridges formed when two or more bowl-like depressions cut into the same mountain	**d.** cirques
_____ **22.** formed when a glacier changes the shape of areas between mountains	**e.** U-shaped valleys

23. Scientists can determine the direction of glacial ice flow by

examining special grooves called _____ .

Types of Glacial Deposits (p. 314)

24. All material carried and deposited by glaciers is called glacial

_____ .

25. On what basis is glacial drift divided into two groups?

_____

_____

26. What are the two types of glacial drift?
   a. kettles and outwash plains
   b. outwash plains and stratified drift
   c. moraines and till
   d. stratified drift and till

Identify each of the following descriptions as *stratified drift* or *till deposits,* and write the correct term in the space provided.

27. _____ Sediment builds around a block of ice and eventually forms a kettle.

28. _____ Melting ice deposits different sizes of rock material.

29. _____ Meltwater streams from glaciers carry a lot of sorted material.

30. _____ Moraines form ridges along the edges of glaciers.

Choose the moraine in Column B that best matches the description in Column A, and write the corresponding letter in the space provided.

Column A	Column B
____ **31.** till that is left beneath a glacier	**a.** medial moraine
____ **32.** eroded rock material dropped at the front of a glacier	**b.** lateral moraine
____ **33.** forms along the sides of a glacier	**c.** ground moraine
____ **34.** forms at the meeting of two different valley glaciers with moraines on each side	**d.** terminal moraine

Review (p. 315)

Now that you've finished Section 3, review what you learned by answering the Review questions in your ScienceLog.

Section 4: Gravity's Effect on Erosion and Deposition (p. 316)

1. Gravity controls mass movement. True or False? (Circle one.)

Angle of Repose (p. 316)

2. Loose material set at the angle of repose _____ slide downslope. (will or will not)

3. Which of the following factors affect the movement of material downslope? (Circle all that apply.)

    a. slope of the resting surface
    b. size of the material
    c. moisture level of the material
    d. weight of the resting surface

▲ **CHAPTER 12**

Rapid Mass Movement (p. 317)

Complete the next section after reading pages 317–318 in the text. Each of the following statements is false. Change the underlined word to make the statement true, and write the correct word in the space provided.

4. A group of loose rocks falling down a steep slope is a <u>landslide</u>.

_____

5. A slump forms when a block of material moves downslope over a(n) <u>angled</u> surface.

_____

6. Mudflows are most common in the mountains when a long, dry season is followed by <u>hot</u> rains.

_____

7. A lahar is a <u>slump</u> that occurs when a volcanic eruption quickly melts a lot of ice, which then mixes with soil and volcanic ash.

_____

Slow Mass Movement (p. 319)

8. More material is moved collectively over time by slow mass movement than by rapid mass movement. True or False? (Circle one.)

9. Which of the following contribute to creep? (Circle all that apply.)
   a. burrowing animals
   b. tree branches acting as wedges between soil particles
   c. rock particles freed by water
   d. plant roots forcing rocks apart

10. Over time, creep can cause tree trunks to bend. True or False? (Circle one.)

Review (p. 319)

Now that you've finished Section 4, review what you learned by answering the Review questions in your ScienceLog.

CHAPTER

13 DIRECTED READING WORKSHEET

Exploring the Oceans

As you read Chapter 13, which begins on page 328 of your textbook, answer the following questions.

Imagine . . . (p. 328)

1. What have the aquanauts of *Aquarius* discovered about the coral on the ocean floor?

   a. The coral is growing much larger than normal.

   b. The coral is becoming an unusual shade of orange.

   c. The coral is damaged by ultraviolet rays.

   d. There is no more coral on the ocean floor.

2. Why are the aquanauts concerned about water pollution?

_____

_____

_____

What Do You Think? (p. 329)

Answer these questions in your ScienceLog now. Then later, you'll have a chance to revise your answers based on what you've learned.

Investigate! (p. 329)

3. What does this activity explain about the *Aquarius*?

_____

_____

_____

Section 1: Earth's Oceans (p. 330)

4. What percentage of the Earth's surface is covered with water?

_____

5. The global ocean is divided by the _____

into four main _____ .

CHAPTER 13

Chapter 13, continued

Divisions of the Global Ocean (p. 330)

Choose the ocean in Column B that is being described in Column A, and write the corresponding letter in the space provided. Answers may be used more than once.

Column A	Column B
_____ **6.** smallest	**a.** Arctic Ocean
_____ **7.** largest	**b.** Pacific Ocean
_____ **8.** contains about one half the water volume of the Pacific Ocean	**c.** Indian Ocean
_____ **9.** home of the mid-ocean ridge	**d.** Atlantic Ocean
_____ **10.** much is covered by ice	

How Did the Oceans Form? (p. 331)

11. How did water vapor collect in the atmosphere before the oceans formed?

   a. It came from another planet.
   b. It came from the sun.
   c. It was spewed from volcanoes.
   d. None of the above

12. What happened to the water vapor when the Earth cooled 3 billion to 3.5 billion years ago? What formed?

_____

_____

The Recent History of Earth's Oceans (p. 331)

13. Place the following statements in chronological order by writing the appropriate number in the space provided.

   _____ All oceans except the Pacific Ocean are expanding.

   _____ The South Atlantic Ocean was much smaller than it is today.

   _____ The Earth had one giant body of water, Panthalassa, and one giant landmass, Pangaea.

   _____ The Indian Ocean and the North Atlantic Ocean began to form.

_____

Chapter 13, continued

Characteristics of Ocean Water (p. 332)

14. Most of the salt in the ocean is the same as the salt we eat.

True or False? (Circle one.)

15. How do minerals on land make the ocean salty?

_____

_____

_____

_____

_____

16. The measure of the amount of dissolved solids in a given

amount of liquid is called salinity. True or False? (Circle one.)

17. Which waters tend to be more saline?
   a. coastal waters in cool, humid environments
   b. river waters
   c. coastal waters in hot, dry climates
   d. coastal waters near river outlets

18. When water evaporates, the dissolved solids in the water also

evaporate. True or False? (Circle one.)

19. Which of the following affect ocean salinity?
(Circle all that apply.)
   a. temperature
   b. humidity
   c. inflow of fresh water
   d. water movement

Use the graph on page 333 to answer questions 20–22.

20. Sunlight only heats the top 100 m of the surface zone. So why
does the surface zone extend to a depth of 300 m?

_____

_____

_____

21. The water in the thermocline has the greatest temperature drop

with increased depth. True or False? (Circle one.)

CHAPTER 13

_____

Chapter 13, continued

_____

22. What two things affect surface-zone temperatures in most regions?

_____

_____

Review (p. 334)

Now that you've finished the first part of Section 1, review what you learned by answering the Review questions in your ScienceLog.

The Ocean and the Water Cycle (p. 335)

23. The water cycle connects all of Earth's _____ ,

_____ , and _____ water together.

Use the diagram on page 335 to choose the term in Column B that best matches the description in Column A, and write the corresponding letter in the space provided.

Column A	Column B
____ **24.** Liquid water is heated by the sun and rises as a gas into the atmosphere.	**a.** precipitation
____ **25.** Droplets fall back to the Earth's surface.	**b.** evaporation
____ **26.** Water vapor cools and turns to liquid water on the dust particles.	**c.** condensation

A Global Thermostat (p. 336)

27. What is an important function of Earth's oceans?

_____

_____

28. Which of the following would happen if the ocean didn't perform this important function? (Circle all that apply.)

a. The average air temperature on Earth would vary more than 200°C from day to night.

b. Rapid heat exchange would cause violent weather patterns.

c. Life as we know it could not exist.

29. How does the circulation of ocean water affect climate?

_____

_____

_____

Review (p. 336)

Now that you've finished Section 1, review what you learned by answering the Review questions in your ScienceLog.

Section 2: The Ocean Floor (p. 337)

1. What have scientists discovered on the ocean floor using state-of-the-art technology?

_____

_____

Exploring the Ocean Floor (p. 337)

2. What is Alvin?

_____

_____

3. What kinds of missions has Alvin been on?

_____

_____

4. Why did the developers of *Deep Flight* give it that name?

_____

_____

_____

Revealing the Ocean Floor (p. 338)

5. The two major regions of land under the water are the

_____ margin and the

_____ basin.

Chapter 13, continued

Use Figure 6 on pages 338–339 to help you answer questions 6–12.
Choose the ocean feature in Column B that is described in Column A,
and write the corresponding letter in the space provided.

Column A	Column B
_____ **6.** begins at the shoreline	**a.** continental rise
_____ **7.** connects the continental shelf with the ocean floor	**b.** abyssal plain
_____ **8.** base of continental slope	**c.** continental shelf
_____ **9.** covered by mud	**d.** continental slope

10. _____ are mountain chains formed by magma coming through rift zones.

11. Mountains on the ocean floor that can turn into volcanic islands are called _____ .

12. _____ are formed where an oceanic plate is forced underneath another plate.

Viewing the Ocean Floor from Above (p. 340)

13. Which of the following are technologies that allow scientists to study the ocean floor without going below the surface? (Circle all that apply.)

   a. sonar   **c.** scuba gear

   b. submarines   **d.** satellites

14. Sonar is based on the behavior of which animal species?

_____

15. How do scientists use sound to figure out the depth of the ocean?

_____

_____

_____

_____

_____

16. How fast does sound travel in water?

_____

Choose the satellite in Column B that was used to study the feature in Column A, and write the corresponding letter in the space provided.

Column A	Column B
_____ **17.** once gathered military intelligence	**a.** *Geosat*
_____ **18.** changes in the height of the ocean's surface	**b.** *Seasat*
_____ **19.** the direction and speed of ocean currents	

20. Using satellites to make maps of the ocean floor is better than using ship-based sonar readings because

    a. satellites are farther away from the ocean.

    b. satellites cover more territory in less time.

    c. ships are always getting lost.

    d. satellites are less expensive.

Review (p. 341)

Now that you've finished Section 2, review what you learned by answering the Review questions in your ScienceLog.

Section 3: Life in the Ocean (p. 342)

1. Marine organisms are divided into _____ main groups.

2. The division of the ocean into two main environments is based

on the _____ living in the environments.

The Three Groups of Marine Life (p. 342)

Use the diagram to choose the group of marine life in Column B that is described in Column A, and write the corresponding letter in the space provided. Groups of marine life may be used more than once.

Column A	Column B
_____ **3.** live on or in the ocean floor	**a.** plankton
_____ **4.** plantlike and animal-like microscopic life	**b.** nekton
_____ **5.** whales and dolphins	**c.** benthos
_____ **6.** free-swimming organisms	
_____ **7.** crabs, worms, and clams	
_____ **8.** drift freely near the ocean surface	

▲▲ **CHAPTER 13**

The Benthic Environment (p. 343)

9. Which of the following is NOT an adaptation of intertidal organisms to their changing environment?

    a. attachment to rocks

    b. alternating tentacles for wet and dry conditions

    c. growing holdfasts that act like roots

    d. having tough shells to protect against waves and harsh sunlight

10. Temperature, water pressure, and amount of sunlight vary widely in the sublittoral zone. True or False? (Circle one.)

11. Why are plants scarce in the bathyal zone?

    _____

    _____

    _____

12. Why do you think tube worms in the abyssal zone live around black smokers?

    _____

    _____

    _____

The Pelagic Environment (p. 345)

Each of the following describes the neritic zone or the oceanic zone. Write *N* for the neritic zone and *O* for the oceanic zone in the space provided.

_____ **13.** covers the entire sea floor except the continental shelf

_____ **14.** covers the continental shelf

_____ **15.** warm and shallow

_____ **16.** home to animals like the anglerfish

_____ **17.** deeper areas have cold water under a lot of pressure

_____ **18.** abundance of sunlight

Review (p. 345)

Now that you've finished Section 3, review what you learned by answering the Review questions in your ScienceLog.

Chapter 13, continued

Section 4: Resources from the Ocean (p. 346)

1. List three resources available in the ocean.

_____

_____

Living Resources (p. 346)

2. Each year, the fishing industry harvests almost

_____ million tons of fish from the ocean.

3. What technologies have helped fishermen increase their harvest?

_____

_____

4. Two recent concerns about the ocean are

_____ and damage to other wildlife from

drift nets.

5. Which of the following is NOT a way to satisfy our demand for
food from the sea?
   a. harvest fish from holding ponds
   b. raise mussels and oysters in offshore nurseries
   c. raise fish in small aquariums
   d. harvest seaweed

6. Why is there seaweed in ice cream?

_____

_____

_____

Nonliving Resources (p. 348)

7. Oil and natural gas are renewable resources. True or False?
(Circle one.)

8. Explain briefly how petroleum engineers find oil and natural gas.

_____

_____

_____

_____

CHAPTER 13

9. If you lived in Saudi Arabia, why might you get your fresh water from a desalination plant?

_____

_____

_____

10. Mineral nodules in the ocean are made mostly of

_____ .

11. Do you want to be a mineral nodule miner? Why or why not?

_____

_____

_____

12. Which of the following are advantages to using tidal energy? (Circle all that apply.)

   a. It's renewable.   **c.** It's clean.

   b. It's practical worldwide.   **d.** It's inexpensive.

13. Look at Figure 20 on page 350. How can water during a high tide be used to generate electricity?

_____

_____

_____

_____

14. If you were in charge of building a wave-energy power plant, where would you build it? Explain.

_____

_____

_____

_____

Review (p. 350)

Now that you've finished Section 4, review what you learned by answering the Review questions in your ScienceLog.

Section 5: Ocean Pollution (p. 351)

1. Humans have used the ocean for waste disposal only during the last 100 years. True or False? (Circle one.)

Sources of Ocean Pollution (p. 351)

2. Why were vials of blood and syringes washing up on beaches in the 1980s?

   _____

   _____

   _____

3. Which statement is NOT true about the solid waste called sludge?

   a. It pollutes beaches and kills marine life.
   b. It contains the solids removed from raw sewage.
   c. It is raw sewage.
   d. It is dumped offshore in the ocean in some areas of the world.

4. How does waste detergent get from your home to the ocean? Number the following steps in order by writing the appropriate number in the space provided.

   _____ Rivers carry the pollution to the ocean.

   _____ The detergent runs off into a stream.

   _____ Streams lead the detergents into rivers.

5. _____ source pollution is the name given to pollution if we can't identify the source.

6. The following are all consequences of the 1989 *Exxon Valdez* oil spill EXCEPT:

   a. Many animals died.
   b. Many Alaskans dependent on fishing lost their businesses.
   c. All Alaskan polar bears turned black.
   d. Alaska's wildlife and economy may suffer for decades.

7. How are oil tankers being built to prevent oil spills?

   _____

   _____

   _____

▲ ▲ ▲
▲ **CHAPTER 13**

Chapter 13, continued

Saving Our Ocean Resources (p. 354)

8. In 1989, _____ countries ratified a treaty

prohibiting the ocean dumping of radioactive wastes, certain

plastics, oil, _____ , and

_____ compounds.

9. Which of the following is NOT an action taken in the United States to decrease ocean pollution?

   a. the Adopt-a-Beach program
   b. the Watergate Relocation Commission
   c. the U.S. Marine Protection, Research, and Sanctuaries Act
   d. the Clean Water Act

10. If you live near a beach, how can you help battle ocean pollution?

_____

_____

_____

_____

_____

Review (p. 355)

Now that you've finished Section 5, review what you learned by answering the Review questions in your ScienceLog.

CHAPTER

14 DIRECTED READING WORKSHEET

The Movement of Ocean Water

As you read Chapter 14, which begins on page 362 of your textbook, answer the following questions.

This Really Happened! (p. 362)

1. Where is the Bermuda Triangle located?

_____

_____

_____

2. Which of the following is NOT a scientific reason why the Bermuda Triangle is feared by sailors?

   a. Large, dangerous waves can be caused by southerly winds.
   b. There are records of supernatural acts in the area.
   c. The wind can die out, leaving ships stranded.
   d. Waterspouts can occur without warning.
   e. Many ships have vanished in the Bermuda Triangle.

What Do You Think? (p. 363)

Answer these questions in your ScienceLog now. Then later, you'll have a chance to revise your answers based on what you've learned.

Investigate! (p. 363)

3. What does this activity demonstrate?

_____

_____

_____

Section 1: Currents (p. 364)

4. Thor Heyerdahl theorized that

   a. Polynesians sailed to Peru on rafts using strong winds and ocean currents.
   b. Peruvians sailed to Polynesia on rafts using strong winds and ocean currents.
   c. strong winds and ocean currents kept the Polynesians from sailing to Peru.
   d. strong winds and ocean currents kept the Peruvians from sailing to Polynesia.

CHAPTER 14

5. What was Thor Heyerdahl trying to prove?

_____

_____

_____

6. How long did it take for Thor Heyerdahl to complete his journey?

_____

_____

Surface Currents (p. 365)

7. The Gulf Stream transports _____ times more water than all the rivers in the world put together.

8. All of the following can affect the formation of surface currents EXCEPT

  a. continental deflection.
  b. the Coriolis effect.
  c. the saltiness of the water.
  d. global winds.

9. Near the North and South Poles, winds blow ocean water

_____ , but near the equator, the current

flows _____ .

10. The Coriolis effect only acts on small objects that turn on an

axis. True or False? (Circle one.)

11. Why don't the Earth's surface currents travel freely across the globe in a uniform pattern?

_____

_____

_____

_____

12. Where do warm-water currents originate?

  a. near the poles
  b. near the equator
  c. on the continents
  d. in the air

Chapter 14, continued

---

13. Take a moment to read the Physics Connection on page 367. What is the initial energy source of ocean surface currents?

_____

_____

Review (p. 367)

Now that you've finished the first part of Section 1, review what you learned by answering the Review questions in your ScienceLog.

Deep Currents (p. 368)

14. Write the density ratio as a fraction. _____

15. a. Deep currents are formed when dense water rises to the surface of the ocean. True or False? (Circle one.)

b. When temperature decreases, the volume of liquid water

_____ . (increases or decreases)

c. Dense water _____ less dense water. (sinks into, floats on)

d. When temperature decreases, the density of liquid water

_____ . (increases or decreases)

16. Put the following events in order to describe how salinity can create deep currents. Starting with 1 for the first event, write the appropriate number in the corresponding space.

_____ Frozen water floats on the ocean surface.

_____ The salinity of the water below the ice increases.

_____ Polar winds chill the ocean water.

_____ The increase in density of the water due to its increased salinity causes the water to sink.

_____ Dissolved solids left behind by the frozen water join the unfrozen water below the ice.

_____ The density of the water below the ice increases due to its higher salinity.

▲ ▲ **CHAPTER 14**

Chapter 14, continued

Mark each of the following statements *True* or *False*. Figures 6 and 7 may help you.

17. _____ It takes 750 days for Antarctic Bottom Water to move from Antarctica's coast to the equator.

18. _____ The North Atlantic Deep Water flows on top of the Antarctic Bottom Water.

19. _____ Deep currents move from polar regions to equatorial regions; warmer surface currents move from equatorial regions to polar regions.

Surface Currents and Climate (p. 370)

Using Figure 8, answer questions 20–21.

20. The California Current carries _____

    water _____ to Mexico.

21. The climate on the West Coast is fairly

    _____ all year long due to the

    _____ .

22. What is upwelling?

    _____

    _____

    _____

    _____

    _____

Mark each of the following statements *True* or *False*.

23. _____ El Niño affects both surface water and the atmosphere.

24. _____ El Niño can occur as often as every 2 to 12 years.

25. _____ El Niño conditions bring heavy rains globally.

Review (p. 371)

Now that you've finished Section 1, review what you learned by answering the Review questions in your ScienceLog.

Chapter 14, continued

Section 2: Waves (p. 372)

1. What is it like to swim in the ocean? If you have never been swimming in the ocean, imagine what it is like.

_____

_____

_____

_____

Anatomy of a Wave (p. 372)

2. What do the letters correspond to on the following diagram?

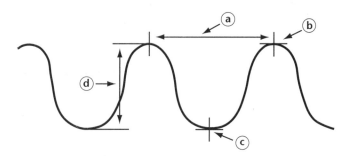

a. _____   c. _____

b. _____   d. _____

Wave Formation and Movement (p. 372)

3. Even though it looks like water moves across the surface in waves, it is actually _____ that is moving through the water.

4. Surface wave energy reaches all the way to the bottom of the ocean. True or False? (Circle one.)

Specifics of Wave Movement (p. 373)

5. In Figure 11, what is the fixed point that is used to measure the period of the wave?

   a. the part of the reef the wave hits first
   b. the bottom of the reef
   c. the reef's peak
   d. None of the above

6. What is the equation for wave speed?

CHAPTER 14

Types of Waves (p. 373)

7. Waves can form by all of the following EXCEPT

   a. wind.
   b. landslides.
   c. the phase of the moon.
   d. impact by cosmic bodies.
   e. earthquakes.

Read pages 373–377. Then, choose the type of wave in Column B that best matches the description in Column A, and write the corresponding letter in the space provided.

Column A	Column B
_____ **8.** interact with the ocean floor	**a.** tsunamis
_____ **9.** caused by the sudden movement of a large volume of ocean water	**b.** shallow-water waves
_____ **10.** break in the open ocean	**c.** deep-water waves
_____ **11.** move in water deeper than one-half their wavelength	**d.** whitecaps

Storm Surges (p. 377)

12. Explain how a storm surge forms.

_____

_____

_____

_____

Review (p. 377)

Now that you've finished Section 2, review what you learned by answering the Review questions in your ScienceLog.

Section 3: Tides (p. 378)

1. Which of the following influence tides? (Circle all that apply.)

   a. Venus
   b. the sun
   c. the moon
   d. Mercury

Chapter 14, continued

2. The sun is the more dominant force affecting the Earth's tides.

True or False? (Circle one.)

The Lure of the Moon (p. 378)

3. Which one of the following is responsible for the theory of gravitational pull?

   a. Lord Kelvin
   b. Marie Curie
   c. Sir Isaac Newton
   d. Pytheas

4. The pull of the moon's gravity is more noticeable in liquids than in solids because liquids are lighter than solids.

True or False? (Circle one.)

5. Where on Earth are you likely to find high tides? (Circle all that apply.)

   a. the part of the Earth that is closest to the moon
   b. the part of the Earth that is directly opposite the part closest to the moon
   c. the part of the Earth that is closest to the sun
   d. any part of the ocean

6. What two factors determine when tides occur?

   _____

   _____

   _____

7. Tides do not occur at the same spots on Earth because

   a. the Earth rotates more quickly than the moon revolves around the Earth.
   b. the moon revolves around the Earth more quickly than the Earth rotates.
   c. the Earth rotates at the same speed that the moon revolves around the Earth.
   d. None of the above

8. How long does it take for a spot on Earth that is facing the moon to rotate so that it is facing the moon again?

   a. 24 hours and 5 minutes
   b. 12 hours and 50 minutes
   c. 12 hours and 5 minutes
   d. 24 hours and 50 minutes

▲▲ CHAPTER 14

Chapter 14, continued

9. Take a moment to read the Brain Food on page 379. How are dry land tides different from ocean tides?

_____

_____

_____

Tidal Variations (p. 380)

10. The difference between the levels of ocean water at high tide and

low tide is called a tidal variation. True or False? (Circle one.)

Read page 380 to determine whether the statements below are true for spring tides or neap tides. Write *ST* for spring tides and *NT* for neap tides in the space provided.

11. _____ occur during the first and third quarters of the moon

12. _____ have the maximum daily tidal range

13. _____ occur when the sun, Earth, and moon are in alignment with one another

14. _____ occur when the sun, Earth, and moon form a 90° angle

15. _____ occur when the sun and the moon's gravitational forces pull on the Earth in the same direction

16. _____ occur when the sun and the moon's gravitational forces pull on the Earth in opposite directions

Tides and Topography (p. 381)

17. Where can a tidal bore occur?

   a. a narrow bay
   b. a wide river
   c. an ocean
   d. a pond

Review (p. 381)

Now that you've finished Section 3, review what you learned by answering the Review questions in your ScienceLog.

CHAPTER

15 DIRECTED READING WORKSHEET

The Atmosphere

As you read Chapter 15, which begins on page 390 of your textbook, answer the following questions.

This Really Happened! (p. 390)

1. What ended Steve Fossett's air balloon flight?

_____

_____

_____

2. What did Fossett do to slow the balloon's fall?

_____

_____

_____

What Do You Think? (p. 391)

Answer these questions in your ScienceLog now. Then later, you'll have a chance to revise your answers based on what you've learned.

Investigate! (p. 391)

3. What is the purpose of this experiment?

_____

_____

_____

Section 1: Characteristics of the Atmosphere (p. 392)

4. Why is the atmosphere important to us? (Circle all that apply.)

    a. It contains the oxygen we breathe.
    b. It keeps the clouds close to the Earth.
    c. It protects us from the sun's harmful rays.
    d. It holds us onto the Earth's surface.

CHAPTER 15

Composition of the Atmosphere (p. 392)

Mark each of the following statements *True* or *False*.

5. _____ The atmosphere contains some solids.

6. _____ Oxygen is the most abundant gas in Earth's atmosphere.

7. _____ Water is the most abundant liquid in Earth's atmosphere.

Atmospheric Pressure and Temperature (p. 393)

8. Why do your ears pop when you ride up or down in an elevator in a tall building?

_____

_____

_____

_____

_____

9. Gravity holds the atmosphere around the Earth.

True or False? (Circle one.)

10. Air pressure ____ _____ as you move away from Earth's sur (increases or decreases)

11. Differences in t ure between layers of the atmosphere are

mainly due to ti _____ is absorbed by gases as it move downward through the atmosphere.

Layers of the Atmosphere (p. 394)

12. In which of the following atmospheric layers does temperature decrease as altitude increases? (Circle all that apply.)

a. troposphere   **c.** mesosphere
b. stratosphere   **d.** thermosphere

13. The pressure of the Earth's atmosphere becomes

_____ _____ as you move away from the Earth's surface. (greater or lesser)

14. Most of the mass of the Earth's atmosphere is in the

_____ _____ . (troposphere or thermosphere)

15. You live in the troposphere. True or False? (Circle one.)

16. Take a look at Figure 5 at the bottom of page 395. Ozone is made up of oxygen atoms. How is ozone different from the oxygen you breathe?

_____

_____

_____

17. The ozone in the atmosphere absorbs _____ . (ultraviolet radiation or gamma rays)

18. The coldest layer of the atmosphere is the

    a. troposphere.   **c.** mesosphere.
    b. stratosphere.   **d.** thermosphere.

19. The thermosphere isn't a hot place, even though it has very high temperatures. Why?

_____

_____

_____

_____

_____

_____

20. Ions are electrically charged particles. True or False? (Circle one.)

21. Ions in the thermosphere are created when

    a. the aurora borealis hits nitrogen atoms.
    b. AM radio waves are absorbed by oxygen atoms.
    c. nitrogen and oxygen atoms absorb solar energy.
    d. meteorites pass through nitrogen and oxygen atoms.

22. There is a definite boundary between the atmosphere and space, called the ionosphere. True or False? (Circle one.)

Review (p. 397)

Now that you've finished Section 1, review what you learned by answering the Review questions in your ScienceLog.

CHAPTER 15

Section 2: Heating of the Atmosphere (p. 398)

1. The Earth's atmosphere is heated by solar energy.
True or False? (Circle one.)

Energy in the Atmosphere (p. 398)

2. The Earth receives about _____ of the
radiation released by the sun.

3. Take a moment to look at Figure 8. What percentage of the sun's
radiation that reaches the Earth is absorbed or reflected in each
of the following ways?

_____ scattered and reflected by clouds and air

_____ reflected by the Earth's surface

_____ absorbed by the Earth's surface

_____ absorbed by ozone, clouds, and atmospheric gases

4. Energy transferred by heat from the sidewalk to your foot is

an example of _____ .
(conduction or convection)

5. In convection currents, cold air _____ .
(sinks or rises)

The Greenhouse Effect (p. 400)

6. Gases in the atmosphere can gain energy from the land and

water. True or False? (Circle one.)

7. Take a look at Figure 10. How do greenhouse gases act like the
layer of glass in a greenhouse?

_____

_____

_____

Mark each of the following statements *True* or *False*.

8. _____ An increase in carbon dioxide might cause global
warming because more carbon dioxide would be
able to trap more heat.

9. _____ The balance between incoming radiation and out-
going heat is called the radiation balance.

10. _____ Rising temperatures on Earth would not cause
major changes in plant and animal communities.

Chapter 15, continued

11. Why would planting millions of trees help reduce the green-house effect?

_____

_____

_____

Review (p. 401)

Now that you've finished Section 2, review what you learned by answering the Review questions in your ScienceLog.

Section 3: Atmospheric Pressure and Winds (p. 402)

1. The damage in Figure 12 was caused by moving air.

True or False? (Circle one.)

Why Air Moves (p. 402)

2. Differences in air pressure create wind. True or False? (Circle one.)

3. The greater the difference is between areas of high and low

pressure, the faster the wind speed. True or False? (Circle one.)

4. _____ air has a higher density than

_____ air.

5. Air pressure is high at the _____ because

the air is _____ there.
(poles or equator, hot or cold)

6. What produces pressure belts?

_____

_____

7. The winds in the Southern Hemisphere curve to the right due to

the Coriolis effect. True or False? (Circle one.)

8. In Figure 15 at the bottom of page 403, what happens if you try to roll a marble across a spinning Lazy Susan?

_____

_____

_____

Types of Winds (p. 404)

9. Which of the following is NOT true of local winds?

 a. They are caused by the uneven heating of the Earth's surface and pressure differences.
 b. They can blow from any direction.
 c. They usually move short distances.
 d. They are part of a pattern of air circulation that moves across the Earth.

Complete the following questions after reading pages 404–406. Be sure to review the figures on those pages.

10. The word *doldrums* comes from an Old English word that means "foolish." Why were the doldrums given that name?

_____

_____

11. The areas of high pressure at 30° north and 30° south latitude are

called the _____ .

12. In the Southern Hemisphere, the westerlies blow from the

southeast to the northwest. True or False? (Circle one.)

13. The polar easterlies in the Northern Hemisphere blow from the

_____ to the _____ .

14. How can knowing about jet streams help a pilot?

_____

_____

Choose the global winds in Column B that best match the description in Column A, and write the corresponding letter in the space provided.

Column A	Column B
____ **15.** winds that blow toward the poles between 30° and 60° latitude in both hemispheres	**a.** polar easterlies
____ **16.** narrow belts of high-speed, high-altitude winds that do not follow regular paths	**b.** westerlies
____ **17.** winds moving from the poles toward 60° latitude in both hemispheres	**c.** northeast trade winds
____ **18.** winds that move from northeast to southwest toward the equator	**d.** jet streams

Chapter 15, continued

Look at Figure 19 on page 406, and then answer the following questions about sea breezes and land breezes.

19. In the afternoon on the beach, after the sun has heated the land,

you can feel _____ breezes. (sea or land)

20. Sea breezes and land breezes are created because air moves from areas of high pressure to areas of low pressure.

True or False? (Circle one.)

Look at Figure 20 on page 407, and then answer the following questions about mountain and valley breezes.

21. In the afternoon in the mountains, after the sun has heated the

valley floor all day, you can feel a _____ breeze. (mountain or valley)

22. Mountain breezes and valley breezes are created because warm

air rises and cold air sinks. True or False? (Circle one.)

Review (p. 407)

Now that you've finished Section 3, review what you learned by answering the Review questions in your ScienceLog.

Section 4: The Air We Breathe (p. 408)

1. Air pollution in cities only became a problem in the twentieth

century. True or False? (Circle one.)

Air Quality (p. 408)

2. Which of the following are natural air pollutants? (Circle all that apply.)

  a. sea salt   **d.** vehicle exhaust fumes
  b. swamp gas   **e.** pollen
  c. smoke from forest fires   **f.** volcanic gases

Types of Air Pollution (p. 409)

3. All primary pollutants are put into the air by humans.

True or False? (Circle one.)

4. Ozone and smog

  a. are made up of automobile exhaust.
  b. are primary pollutants.
  c. are formed when automobile exhaust reacts with sunlight.
  d. are formed when automobile exhaust reacts with water.

CHAPTER 15

Sources of Human-Caused Air Pollution (p. 410)

5. The main source of human-caused air pollution today is

_____ . (transportation or industry)

6. The burning of fossil fuels releases large amounts of oxides into
the air. True or False? (Circle one.)

7. List three things that contribute to indoor air pollution.

_____

_____

_____

The Air Pollution Problem (p. 411)

Mark each of the following statements *True* or *False*.

8. _____ Pollution always stays in the area where it is released.

9. _____ Acid precipitation can kill trees and fish.

10. _____ The ozone hole is dangerous because it allows more
UV radiation to reach the Earth.

11. Which of the following are possible effects of air pollution on
the human body? (Circle all that apply.)

  a. lung cancer   **c.** coughing
  b. burning eyes   **d.** runny nose

Cleaning Up Our Act (p. 412)

12. The EPA can control the amount of air pollutants that can be
released from any human-controlled source.

True or False? (Circle one.)

13. The EPA has set a standard for the amount of

_____ that comes out of the

_____ on new cars.

14. How many tons of ash do scrubbers remove each year from the
smokestacks of coal-burning plants?

_____

Review (p. 413)

Now that you've finished Section 4, review what you learned by
answering the Review questions in your ScienceLog.

16 · DIRECTED READING WORKSHEET

Understanding Weather

As you read Chapter 16, which begins on page 420 of your textbook, answer the following questions.

Would You Believe . . . ? (p. 420)

1. Where is Tornado Alley? Name the states that are part of Tornado Alley.

_____

_____

_____

What Do You Think? (p. 421)

Answer these questions in your ScienceLog now. Then later, you'll have a chance to revise your answers based on what you've learned.

Investigate! (p. 421)

2. What is the purpose of this investigation?

_____

_____

Section 1: Water in the Air (p. 422)

3. Rainbows form when _____ break up sunlight into different colors.

The Water Cycle (p. 422)

4. When plants release water vapor into the air through their leaves they are experiencing _____ .

5. Water that flows across land and collects in rivers, streams, and the ocean is called _____ .

6. _____ is the transformation of liquid water into water vapor.

7. Rain, snow, sleet, and hail are all forms of
    a. condensation.   **c.** precipitation.
    b. transpiration.   **d.** evaporation.

Humidity (p. 423)

8. What makes straight hair become curly and curly hair become frizzy on bad hair days? Explain.

_____

_____

_____

9. What kind of air holds the highest amount of water vapor?
   a. warmer air
   b. moderate air
   c. cooler air
   d. drier air

10. Relative humidity compares the amount of moisture in the air

with the _____ amount of moisture that the air can hold at a certain temperature.
(maximum or minimum)

11. If the temperature drops but the amount of water vapor in the air stays the same, the relative humidity

_____ . (increases or decreases)

12. On a psychrometer, if there is little humidity in the air, there will

be a _____ drop in the temperature of the wet-bulb thermometer. (large or small)

13. Look at "Follow the Numbers" on page 424. If you use a psychrometer and obtain a dry-bulb reading of 12°C and a wet-bulb reading of 11°C, the relative humidity table shows a relative

humidity of _____ .

The Process of Condensation (p. 425)

14. Why do water droplets form on the outside of a glass of ice water?

_____

_____

15. When air cools to a temperature at which it is completely saturated with water, we say that the air has reached its

_____ .

Review (p. 425)

Now that you've finished the first part of Section 1, review what you learned by answering the Review questions in your ScienceLog.

Chapter 16, continued

Clouds (p. 426)

16. What is a cloud made of?

_____

_____

Choose the word in Column B that best matches the definition in Column A, and write the corresponding letter in the space provided.

Column A	Column B
_____ **17.** cloud that forms in layers	**a.** fog
_____ **18.** puffy, white cloud with a flat bottom	**b.** nimbostratus
_____ **19.** cloud that forms near the ground	**c.** stratus
_____ **20.** cloud that produces thunderstorms	**d.** cirrus
_____ **21.** cloud that produces light, continuous rain	**e.** cumulonimbus
_____ **22.** thin, feathery, high-altitude cloud	**f.** cumulus

23. In Figure 8 the prefixes *cirro-*, *alto-*, and *strato-* classify clouds by their

a. temperature.   **c.** size.
b. shape.   **d.** altitude.

Precipitation (p. 428)

24. A water droplet in a cloud becomes rain when its diameter increases to about _____ its normal size and becomes too heavy to stay in the cloud.

a. 2 times   **c.** 100 times
b. 10 times   **d.** 1,000 times

Mark each of the following statements *True* or *False*.

25. _____ The most common form of solid precipitation is hail.

26. _____ Sleet is melted ice.

27. _____ Hail can move both up and down in clouds.

28. _____ The water content of snow is determined by weighing the snow.

Review (p. 429)

Now that you've finished Section 1, review what you learned by answering the Review questions in your ScienceLog.

Section 2: Air Masses and Fronts (p. 430)

1. What causes changes in the weather?

_____

_____

Air Masses (p. 430)

2. What two characteristics of air masses are represented with the two-letter symbol on weather maps?

   a. density and moisture   **c.** moisture and temperature

   b. mass and temperature   **d.** shape and mass

3. On weather maps, a two-letter symbol system describes the characteristics of air masses. Give the four letters used in this system, and tell what each letter represents.

_____

_____

_____

4. Where do the air masses that are responsible for cold, winter weather in the United States come from? (Circle all that apply.)

   a. Canada   **c.** the North Atlantic Ocean

   b. the North Pacific Ocean   **d.** Mexico

5. Of the four warm air masses that influence the weather in the United States, how many develop over land?

_____

6. Which air masses cause the hurricanes that occur on the East Coast of the United States?

_____

_____

Fronts (p. 432)

7. What is the weather like at a front?

   a. clear and calm   **c.** cloudy and stormy

   b. warm and dry   **d.** cold and dry

8. Take a moment to read the Brain Food on page 432. Meteorologists first started using the term *front* to describe weather phenomena during World War I. They compared air masses to opposing

   a. armies.   **c.** submarines.

   b. tanks.   **d.** machine guns.

Chapter 16, continued

Choose the type of front in Column B that best matches the description in Column A, and write the corresponding letter in the space provided.

Column A	Column B
____ **9.** A warm air mass overrides a cold air mass.	**a.** cold front
____ **10.** A cold air mass overtakes a warm air mass and then meets a cold air mass.	**b.** warm front
____ **11.** A cold air mass meets and displaces a warm air mass.	**c.** occluded front
____ **12.** Little horizontal movement occurs.	**d.** stationary front

Review (p. 433)

Now that you've finished Section 2, review what you learned by answering the Review questions in your ScienceLog.

Section 3: Severe Weather (p. 434)

1. Name three examples of severe weather.

_____

Thunderstorms (p. 434)

2. Which one of the following atmospheric conditions produces thunderstorms?

   a. The air near the Earth's surface is warm and moist.
   b. The air near the Earth's surface is cold and dry.
   c. The atmosphere is stable.
   d. The atmosphere is bright.

3. Which type of a cloud would most likely lead you to predict a thunderstorm?

   a. a stratus cloud   **c.** a cumulus cloud
   b. a cirrus cloud   **d.** a cumulonimbus cloud

Mark each of the following statements *True* or *False*.

4. _____ Lightning occurs when there is a difference in charge between two surfaces.

5. _____ Thunder results from the expansion of air along the lightning strike.

6. _____ Sudden flash flooding is the biggest cause of weather-related deaths.

7. _____ All thunderstorms produce lightning.

Tornadoes (p. 436)

8. What is the relationship between a funnel cloud and a tornado?

_____

_____

Indicate the correct order for the steps in the formation of a tornado by writing the appropriate number in the space provided.

9. _____ The column of rotating air travels to the base of the cumulonimbus cloud.

10. _____ Strong updrafts of air turn the column of rotating air to a vertical position.

11. _____ The funnel cloud touches the ground.

12. _____ A layer of air between winds traveling in two directions rotates like a roll of toilet paper.

13. Look at the Brain Food on page 437. What do you call a tornado that occurs over water?

a. an aqueous tornado   **c.** a whirlpool
b. a water funnel   **d.** a waterspout

14. In what seasons do most tornadoes in the United States occur?

a. late summer and fall   **c.** spring and early summer
b. late fall and winter   **d.** winter and early spring

15. Why are tornadoes so dangerous?

_____

_____

_____

Hurricanes (p. 437)

16. Hurricanes that form over the western Pacific Ocean are called

_____ , while those that begin in the

Indian Ocean are called _____ .

17. Hurricanes rotate in opposite directions in the Northern and

Southern Hemispheres. True or False? (Circle one.)

18. Where does the energy that fuels a hurricane come from?

_____

_____

Choose the term in Column B that best matches the description in Column A, and write the corresponding letter in the space provided.

Column A	Column B
____ **19.** clouds that spiral around the center of a hurricane	**a.** eye
____ **20.** cumulonimbus clouds that produce strong winds and heavy rains	**b.** eye wall
____ **21.** core of warm, calm air	**c.** rain bands

22. What causes most of the damage associated with hurricanes?

    a. flooding   **c.** cold weather

    b. high winds   **d.** lightning

23. Look at the Astronomy Connection on page 439. On Jupiter storms can last decades or even centuries! The Great Red Spot of Jupiter is most like a(n)

    a. hurricane.   **c.** thunderstorm.

    b. tornado.   **d.** air mass.

Review (p. 439)

Now that you've finished Section 3, review what you learned by answering the Review questions in your ScienceLog.

Section 4: Forecasting the Weather (p. 440)

1. Why is it important to be able to predict the weather?

_____

_____

Weather Forecasting Technology (p. 440)

Write the name of the tool used to measure each atmospheric condition in the space provided.

2. wind direction _____

3. air pressure _____

4. air temperature _____

5. wind speed _____

6. What two substances are used in liquid thermometers like the one in Figure 26?

_____

7. An anemometer is a glass tube sealed at one end and placed in a container of mercury. True or False? (Circle one.)

8. What kind of information do meteorologists get from weather balloons?

_____

_____

_____

Mark each of the following statements *True* or *False*.

9. _____ Radar cannot distinguish between storms of differing intensities.

10. _____ Radar can be used to detect tornadoes.

11. _____ Weather satellites can determine temperatures at various altitudes.

Weather Maps (p. 442)

12. Give the full name and initials of two major sources of weather data in the United States.

_____

_____

_____

_____

13. Similar to contour lines on a topographical map,

_____ connect points of equal

_____ on a weather map.

14. What does an isobar that is a closed circle represent?

_____

_____

Review (p. 443)

Now that you've finished Section 4, review what you learned by answering the Review questions in your ScienceLog.

CHAPTER

17 DIRECTED READING WORKSHEET

Climate

As you read Chapter 17, which begins on page 450 of your textbook, answer the following questions.

What If . . .? (p. 450)

1. Why do you need summer clothes, rain gear, and a down-filled jacket on a three-day trip to climb Mount Kilimanjaro?

_____

_____

_____

_____

2. The climate changes as one travels from the equator to the poles.

   True or False? (Circle one.)

What Do You Think? (p. 451)

Answer these questions in your ScienceLog now. Then later, you'll have a chance to revise your answers based on what you've learned.

Investigate! (p. 451)

3. How does the angle of the sun's rays affect climate?

_____

_____

_____

_____

Section 1: What Is Climate? (p. 452)

4. When you step outside to see if there are rain clouds in

   the sky, you are checking the _____ .
   (weather or climate)

5. If you look through your town's records for average temperature and rainfall over the past 10 years, you are looking at

   _____ data. (weather or climate)

Latitude (p. 453)

Mark each of the following statements *True* or *False*.

6. _____ Latitude is a measure of how far a place is from the equator.

7. _____ The amount of solar energy that a particular area receives is determined, in part, by its latitude.

8. _____ The sun makes a smaller angle with the Earth at lower latitudes.

9. Look at Figure 4 in the middle of page 454. During June and July, why is it summer in the Northern Hemisphere and winter in the Southern Hemisphere?

_____

_____

_____

_____

_____

_____

_____

_____

Prevailing Winds (p. 455)

10. As cold air is heated, it can hold _____

water vapor. As warm air rises, it _____ .
(more or less, warms or cools)

11. There will probably be more precipitation in an area if the prevailing winds are

a. warm and dry.   **c.** warm and moist.
b. cold and dry.   **d.** cold and moist.

12. Winds tend to be drier if they blow across land. True or False? (Circle one.)

13. According to Figure 6 at the bottom of page 455, the prevailing winds that blow across the Sahara Desert are formed from warm,

dry, sinking air. True or False? (Circle one.)

Chapter 17, continued

Geography (p. 456)

14. Mount Kilimanjaro is located very close to the equator. Why is Kilimanjaro always snowy and cold at the top?

_____

_____

_____

_____

_____

Look at Figure 7. Put the steps of rain-shadow formation in the correct order by writing the corresponding number in the appropriate space.

15. _____ Air crosses the mountains and begins to sink.

16. _____ Air cools and releases moisture.

17. _____ Air warms and absorbs moisture.

18. _____ Air rises as it meets mountains.

19. _____ Air produces a desert.

Ocean Currents (p. 457)

20. Which one of the following statements about surface currents is NOT true?

    a. They can move along the coastlines.
    b. They are always warm.
    c. They influence an area's climate.
    d. They occur near the surface of the ocean.

21. Why does southern Iceland have milder temperatures than Greenland?

_____

_____

_____

_____

_____

Review (p. 457)

Now that you've finished Section 1, review what you learned by answering the Review questions in your ScienceLog.

Section 2: Climates of the World (p. 458)

1. What does climate have to do with the kinds of animals that live in an area?

_____

_____

_____

2. Look at Figure 10. All of the following are biomes in Africa EXCEPT
   a. tropical rain forest.
   b. tropical savanna.
   c. tropical desert.
   d. tundra.

The Tropical Zone (p. 459)

3. The tropical zone, which is located around the equator, receives

   the most _____ .
   (solar radiation or annual rainfall)

Mark each of the following statements *True* or *False*.

4. _____ Some trees in the tropical rain forests use above-ground roots to capture more moisture.

5. _____ Tropical deserts can get as hot as 50°C.

6. _____ In the tropical savanna, some seeds need fire to break open their outer skin.

After you finish reading pages 458–461, choose the biome in Column B that best matches the description given in Column A, and write the corresponding letter in the space provided. Biomes may be used more than once.

Column A	Column B
____ 7. soil is poor in organic matter	a. tropical rain forest
____ 8. thin and nutrient-poor soil	b. tropical savanna
____ 9. vegetation includes succulents	c. tropical desert
____ 10. vegetation includes 3–5 m tall grasses	
____ 11. vegetation includes bamboo	
____ 12. soil is enriched by frequent grass fires	

Review (p. 461)

Now that you've finished the first part of Section 2, review what you learned by answering the Review questions in your ScienceLog.

Chapter 17, continued

The Temperate Zone (p. 462)

13. The continental United States is in the climate zone

between the _____ and the

_____ .

14. Deciduous trees keep their leaves year-round. True or False? (Circle one.)

15. All evergreen trees have needle-shaped leaves. True or False? (Circle one.)

16. In North America, temperate grasslands are called

    a. prairies.   **c.** veldt.

    b. pampas.   **d.** steppes.

17. Temperate grassland makes good cropland because it is so

_____ .

18. How is chaparral vegetation similar to tropical savanna vegetation?

_____

_____

19. The main difference between tropical and temperate deserts is that

    a. temperate deserts get less that 25 cm of rain each year.

    b. tropical deserts get very hot in the daytime.

    c. no succulents live in temperate deserts.

    d. temperate deserts get very cold at night.

20. It often snows during the winter in temperate deserts.

True or False? (Circle one.)

The Polar Zone (p. 464)

21. Temperatures in the polar zone are always below freezing, even

in the summer. True or False? (Circle one.)

22. Take a moment to read the Environment Connection in the right column of page 465. Why did John Torrington's body look almost the same in 1984 as it did when he died, in the 1840s?

_____

_____

_____

▲ **CHAPTER 17**

After you finish reading pages 465–466, decide whether each of the following statements is true for *tundra* or for *taiga*, and write the correct biome in the space provided.

23. _____ This biome contains many pine, spruce, and fir trees.

24. _____ This biome has a permanently frozen layer of soil.

25. _____ Of these two biomes, this one is the farther south.

26. _____ Polar bears live in this biome.

27. _____ In the winter, it has almost 24 hours of night.

28. _____ Only deserts are drier than this biome.

29. _____ This biome has acidic soil.

Microclimates (p. 466)

30. An area of tundra or taiga can exist at high elevations in the tropics. True or False? (Circle one.)

31. Why are cities considered microclimates?

_____

_____

_____

_____

_____

Review (p. 466)

Now that you've finished Section 2, review what you learned by answering the Review questions in your ScienceLog.

Section 3: Changes in Climate (p. 467)

1. Would you notice a change in climate? Why or why not?

_____

_____

_____

2. Humans can influence climatic change. True or False? (Circle one.)

Chapter 17, continued

Ice Ages (p. 467)

3. The period of cold during an ice age when much of the Earth's surface becomes covered by ice is called a

_____ period. (interglacial or glacial)

4. Sea level _____ during an interglacial period. (rises or falls)

Match the change in the Earth's axis or tilt in Column B with the effect on the Earth's climate in Column A, and write the corresponding letter in the space provided.

Column A	Column B
____ **5.** not as much seasonal change	**a.** Earth's axis traces a circle every 26,000 years.
____ **6.** determines the time of year when Earth is closest to the sun	**b.** Every 41,000 years, the Earth's axis is tilted at 24.4°.
____ **7.** poles receive more solar energy	**c.** Earth's orbit is a more circular shape.
____ **8.** hotter summers and cooler winters	**d.** Earth's orbit is a more elliptical shape.

9. Do volcanic eruptions affect the Earth's climate? Explain.

_____

_____

_____

_____

_____

10. Plate tectonics have no effect on the Earth's climate.

True or False? (Circle one.)

11. Ice ages may occur when the continents are closer to

_____ regions. (polar or tropical)

CHAPTER 17

Chapter 17, continued

Global Warming (p. 470)

12. Sometimes it is hotter inside a car than outside. Why?

_____

_____

_____

_____

_____

13. In the greenhouse effect, greenhouse gases, such as

_____ , trap heat inside the Earth's
atmosphere.

14. How does the burning of trees, shown in Figure 31 on page 471, contribute to global warming?

_____

_____

_____

_____

_____

15. Which of the following is NOT a predicted consequence of global warming?

   a. The Midwest will become colder and wetter.

   b. Sea level will rise.

   c. Canada's farming conditions will improve.

   d. Coastal areas will experience flooding.

Review (p. 471)

Now that you've finished Section 3, review what you learned by answering the Review questions in your ScienceLog.

Observing the Sky

As you read Chapter 18, which begins on page 480 of your textbook, answer the following questions.

Imagine . . . (p. 480)

1. The Hubble Space Telescope is carried back and forth into space on each space shuttle mission. True or False? (Circle one.)

What Do You Think? (p. 481)

Answer these questions in your ScienceLog now. Then later, you'll have a chance to revise your answers based on what you've learned.

Investigate! (p. 481)

2. What will you learn to measure in this activity?

_____

_____

Section 1: Astronomy—The Original Science (p. 482)

3. What did ancient cultures base their calendars on?

_____

_____

The Stars and Keeping Time (p. 482)

Choose the word in Column B that best matches the description in Column A, and write the corresponding letter in the space provided.

Column A	Column B
____ **4.** the time required for the moon to orbit once around the Earth	**a.** calendar
____ **5.** the time required for Earth to orbit once around the sun	**b.** day
____ **6.** the time required for Earth to rotate once on its axis	**c.** month
____ **7.** a system for organizing time	**d.** year

8. The ancient Egyptian calendar contained one 5-day month.

True or False? (Circle one.)

9. Which ancient calendars were linked to the sun?
(Circle all that apply.)

    a. Mayan   **c.** Chinese

    b. Egyptian   **d.** Hebrew

10. Why did Julius Caesar add 90 days to the year 45 B.C.?

    _____

    _____

11. Leap years are necessary because all months do not have the

same number of days. True or False? (Circle one.)

12. Most countries use the _____ calendar.

    a. Gregorian   **c.** Roman

    b. Julian   **d.** American

Early Observers—Beginnings of Astronomy (p. 484)

Read pp. 484 and 485, and then complete the following section.
Match each site or culture in Column B with the correct description
in Column A, and write the corresponding letter in the space
provided. One term from Column B will be used twice.

Column A	Column B
____ **13.** invented algebra and our modern number system	**a.** Nabta
____ **14.** the earliest record of astronomical observations	**b.** Stonehenge
____ **15.** made an accurate calendar based on skilled forecasting	**c.** the Babylonians
____ **16.** could predict eclipses	**d.** the ancient Chinese
____ **17.** used logic and geometry to explain eclipses and the phases of the moon	**e.** the ancient Greeks
____ **18.** some stones in circles are aligned with the sunrise during the solstices	**f.** the Maya
____ **19.** many buildings are aligned with celestial bodies during certain astronomical events	**g.** the ancient Arabs
____ **20.** produced the world's oldest existing portable star map	

Chapter 18, continued

21. While Europe was in the Dark Ages, the Arab culture continued
    to develop astronomy. True or False? (Circle one.)

The Who's Who of Early Astronomy (p. 486)

22. How did the earliest astronomers learn what they knew about
    the universe?

    _____

    _____

    _____

23. How long did Ptolemy's Earth-centered theory remain the popu-
    lar theory for the structure of the universe?
    a. 100 years   **c.** 1,500 years
    b. 500 years   **d.** 5,000 years

24. Copernicus thought that the planets orbit

    _____ and _____

    was at the center of the universe.
    (Earth or the sun, Earth or the sun)

Choose the name of the scientist in Column B that best matches
the description in Column A, and write the corresponding letter in
the space provided. One scientist from Column B will be used twice.

Column A	Column B
____ **25.** explained that planets and moons stay in orbit due to gravity	**a.** Galileo
____ **26.** stated that planets move in elliptical orbits around the sun	**b.** Tycho Brahe
____ **27.** used a mural quadrant to measure the positions of planets and stars	**c.** Johannes Kepler
____ **28.** was the first person to use a telescope to observe celestial bodies	**d.** Sir Isaac Newton
____ **29.** discovered sunspots	

Modern Astronomy (p. 488)

30. Which planet did William Herschel discover in 1781?
    a. Uranus   **c.** Mars
    b. Jupiter   **d.** Pluto

CHAPTER 18

31. Which invention in the 1800s allowed astronomers to improve their observations of the sky?

    a. the telescope   **c.** the telegraph

    b. photography   **d.** filters

32. Edwin Hubble discovered that the "fuzzy patches" observed by William Herschel were really other

    _____ .

Review (p. 488)

Now that you've finished Section 1, review what you learned by answering the Review questions in your ScienceLog.

Section 2: Mapping the Stars (p. 489)

1. How did ancient cultures name the stars in the sky?

_____

_____

_____

2. If people in ancient cultures could see our modern sky, they would see the same patterns of stars that we do. True or False? (Circle one.)

Constellations (p. 489)

3. What are constellations?

_____

_____

_____

_____

4. The ancient Greek constellation _____ was the same as the Japanese constellation of a drum.

5. The sky is divided into a total of _____ constellations by modern astronomers.

6. Why do astronomers around the world use the same names for the constellations?

_____

_____

7. The constellations that are visible in the sky are different in the spring and the fall. True or False? (Circle one.)

Finding Stars in the Night Sky (p. 491)

Read pp. 491 and 492, and then complete the following section. Choose the word in Column B that best matches the description in Column A, and write the corresponding letter in the space provided. One term from Column B will be used twice.

Column A	Column B
_____ **8.** imaginary point directly over the head of the observer	**a.** zenith
_____ **9.** position of a star in degrees north or south of the celestial equator	**b.** celestial equator
_____ **10.** imaginary extension of Earth's equator into space	**c.** horizon
_____ **11.** angle between an object and the horizon	**d.** altitude
_____ **12.** always 90° from the zenith	**e.** right ascension
_____ **13.** where the sun appears on the first day of spring	**f.** declination
_____ **14.** measure of how far east an object is from where the sun appears on the vernal equinox	**g.** vernal equinox
_____ **15.** line where the sky and Earth appear to meet	

16. Some stars located near Earth's poles can be seen year-round, at all times of night. What are these stars called?

_____

The Size and Scale of the Universe (p. 493)

17. Copernicus reasoned that the stars must be very far from planets because their relative positions shift. True or False? (Circle one.)

18. Look at the Physics Connection. What does red shift tell us about other galaxies?

_____

_____

_____

19. A light-year is equal to the distance that light travels through

space in _____ year(s).

20. One light-year is about 9.46 trillion

_____ .

21. What does Figure 17 show you about the stars in a constellation?
   a. They are spaced apart evenly.
   b. They are fairly close together.
   c. They are equal distances from Earth.
   d. They are very far away from each other.

22. Most stars are smaller than Earth. True or False? (Circle one.)

Use the diagrams on pp. 494 and 495 to help you complete items 23 and 24.

23. At what distance from Earth would our entire solar system be visible from space?
   a. 100 km   **c.** 150 light-days
   b. 1,000,000 km   **d.** 10 light-years

24. The universe looks _____ at a distance of 10 million light-years. (crowded or empty)

Review (p. 495)

Now that you've finished Section 2, review what you learned by answering the Review questions in your ScienceLog.

Section 3: Telescopes—Then and Now (p. 496)

1. What do telescopes do with electromagnetic radiation?

_____

_____

Optical Astronomy (p. 496)

2. The simplest telescope contains two lenses—an objective lens and

a lens located in the _____ of the telescope.

3. As many as _____ stars are visible in the sky without a telescope.

Chapter 18, continued

4. Why do most professional astronomers use reflecting telescopes?

_____

_____

_____

_____

5. Which of the following is NOT true of reflecting telescopes?
   a. They use curved mirrors to collect light.
   b. Flaws in the glass don't affect the collected light.
   c. Different colors of light are focused in one place.
   d. Lenses gather and focus light.

6. Why is a mountaintop the best place on Earth to put a telescope?

_____

_____

_____

7. The clearest images of objects in deep space are produced by a telescope in space. True or False? (Circle one.)

Non-Optical Astronomy (p. 499)

8. Our bodies sense infrared radiation as

_____ .

9. James Clerk Maxwell discovered that light is a form of

_____ radiation.

Each of the following wavelengths is either blocked or unblocked by the Earth's atmosphere. In the space provided, write *B* if the wavelength is blocked and *U* if the wavelength is unblocked.

10. _____ infrared radiation

11. _____ radio waves

12. _____ gamma rays

13. _____ X rays

▲ **CHAPTER 18**

14. A different type of telescope or _____ is needed for each type of electromagnetic radiation.

15. In Figure 24, what is the cloudlike object that goes across each picture?

_____

_____

Mark each of the following statements *True* or *False.*

16. _____ Optical telescopes are much larger than radio telescopes.

17. _____ Small quantities of radio radiation reach Earth from objects in space.

18. Why can chicken wire be used as the surface of a radio telescope?

_____

_____

_____

_____

19. In the _____

_____ _____ , many radio telescopes are linked to work as one giant telescope.

20. The Chandra telescope is the most powerful infrared telescope ever built. True or False? (Circle one.)

Review (p. 501)

Now that you've finished Section 3, review what you learned by answering the Review questions in your ScienceLog.

CHAPTER

19 ▚ **DIRECTED READING WORKSHEET**

Formation of the Solar System

As you read Chapter 19, which begins on page 508 of your textbook, answer the following questions.

Imagine . . . (p. 508)

1. What kind of gravity would you experience on a space station? Explain.

_____

_____

_____

_____

2. Where could you practice "flying" in a rotating space station?

   a. along the perimeter   **c.** on the floor of the station

   b. at the central axis   **d.** None of the above

What Do You Think? (p. 509)

Answer these questions in your ScienceLog now. Then later, you'll have a chance to revise your answers based on what you've learned.

Investigate! (p. 509)

3. What will you be observing in this activity?

_____

_____

_____

Section 1: A Solar System Is Born (p. 510)

4. The Earth, _____ other planets, and the

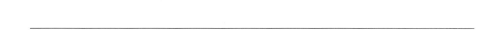 _____ make up most of our solar system.

▲ ▲ CHAPTER 19

The Solar Nebula (p. 510)

Mark each of the following statements *True* or *False*.

5. _____ Nebulas are huge interstellar clouds consisting mostly of dust, helium, and hydrogen.

6. _____ Nebulas are the first ingredient for building a new planetary system.

7. _____ In a dense nebula, the strong attraction between the dust and gas particles can pull the mass to the center of the nebula.

8. _____ An increase in temperature results when the gas molecules in a nebula slow down.

9. In Figure 2, how do gravity and pressure keep the gas molecules in balance in a nebula?

_____

_____

_____

_____

_____

10. Which event does NOT cause the formation of a solar nebula?
    a. Something disturbs the balance between pressure and gravity.
    b. Two nebulas crash.
    c. Gas molecules crash between two stars.
    d. A nearby star explodes.

From Planetesimals to Planets (p. 512)

11. Place the following statements in the correct sequence for the formation of a solar system. Figure 3 may help you.

    _____ Dust and clouds of a nebula collapse.

    _____ Planetesimals sweep up dust and gas to form planets.

    _____ Remaining dust and gas are removed from the solar system.

    _____ The nebula flattens into a disk and warms at its center.

    _____ Dust sticks together and forms planetesimals.

12. How did the gas planets form?

_____

_____

_____

_____

_____

13. The sun's temperature caused planets near the sun to lose their

    a. hydrogen and helium.   **c.** moons and rings.

    b. rocky material.   **d.** None of the above

14. Where can we find evidence of violent collisions of planetesimals?

_____

15. The center of the solar nebula reached temperatures hot enough

to cause hydrogen _____ .

Review (p. 514)

Now that you've finished the first part of Section 1, review what you learned by answering the Review questions in your ScienceLog.

Planetary Motion (p. 515)

16. The planets in the solar system move according to strict physical laws. True or False? (Circle one.)

Choose the definition in Column B that best matches the term in Column A, and write the corresponding letter in the space provided.

Column A	Column B
_____ **17.** orbit	**a.** time it takes for a body to travel once through its path
_____ **18.** rotation	**b.** spinning on an axis
_____ **19.** period of revolution	**c.** motion of a less massive body in its path around a more massive body
_____ **20.** revolution	**d.** path of a body traveling around a larger body

▲▲ CHAPTER 19

21. The Earth rotates around the sun. True or False? (Circle one.)

22. Why do you suppose the planets don't go flying off into space?

_____

_____

_____

_____

_____

23. What did Kepler observe about the movement of Mars?
   a. It has a circular orbit.
   b. Its moons have different orbits.
   c. It had an ellipse-shaped orbit.
   d. None of the above

Mark each of the following statements *True* or *False*.

24. _____ One astronomical unit (AU) is about 150 million kilometers.

25. _____ Distances from the Earth to other planets can be given in AUs rather than kilometers.

26. _____ Planets move faster when they're far from the sun, and they move slower when they're close to the sun.

27. _____ The time it takes for a planet to travel around the sun can be used to calculate the planet's average distance from the sun.

Newton's Law of Universal Gravitation (p. 517)

28. What question was Kepler unable to answer?

_____

_____

29. Newton provided an explanation of how gravity works.

   True or False? (Circle one.)

30. Newton's universal law of gravitation tells us that the effect

   of _____ on an object depends on
   the distance from another object and the

   _____ of each object·

31. Moving two objects away from each other

_____ the gravitational attraction between them. (increases or decreases)

32. Because of its velocity and the pull of gravity, the moon stays in orbit around the Earth. True or False? (Circle one.)

Review (p. 518)

Now that you've finished Section 1, review what you learned by answering the Review questions in your ScienceLog.

Section 2: The Sun: Our Very Own Star (p. 519)

1. How is our sun like the other stars in our galaxy?

_____

_____

_____

The Structure of the Sun (p. 519)

2. The sun has a solid surface. True or False? (Circle one.)

3. List the layers of the sun in order from innermost to outermost.

_____

_____

Match each of the terms in Column B with the correct description in Column A, and write the corresponding letter in the space provided. Figure 9 may help you.

Column A	Column B
_____ **4.** where the sun's energy is produced	**a.** core
_____ **5.** the sun's outer atmosphere	**b.** radiative zone
_____ **6.** where atoms are very closely packed	**c.** convective zone
_____ **7.** where hot and cool gases meet	**d.** photosphere
_____ **8.** only visible during a solar eclipse; deep red	**e.** chromosphere
_____ **9.** the layer of the sun we see	**f.** corona
_____ **10.** can extend outward 10–12 times the sun's diameter	

▲▲ CHAPTER 19

Energy Production in the Sun (p. 520)

11. Which of the following are incorrect explanations for the source of the sun's energy? (Circle all that apply.)

    a. The sun is burning fuel to create the heat.
    b. The sun is shrinking.
    c. The sun is bright and hot because of nuclear energy.

12. What did Einstein discover about matter and energy?

_____

_____

13. Einstein's formula states that energy equals

    a. mass times the speed of light.
    b. mass times the square of the particles of light.
    c. mass times the square of the speed of light.

14. The source of the sun's energy is _____ .

Mark each of the following statements *True* or *False*.

15. _____ In the extreme temperatures of the sun, the repulsive force in atoms is stronger than the attractive force.

16. _____ In nuclear fission, helium turns into hydrogen.

17. _____ The energy released in nuclear fusion is immediately converted into light that leaves the sun.

18. _____ Deuterium is a heavy form of hydrogen.

Activity on the Sun's Surface (p. 522)

19. Sunspots are not really "spots" on the sun. What are they?

_____

_____

_____

20. The number of sunspots on our sun

    a. is steadily decreasing.
    b. remains the same each year.
    c. changes in a regular cycle.
    d. is steadily increasing.

21. Solar flares are giant _____ on the sun's surface.

22. What are auroras?

_____

_____

_____

_____

Review (p. 523)

Now that you've finished Section 2, review what you learned by answering the Review questions in your ScienceLog.

Section 3: The Earth Takes Shape (p. 524)

1. How is studying the Earth's early history like trying to put together a huge jigsaw puzzle?

_____

_____

_____

The Solid Earth Takes Form (p. 524)

Fill in the empty boxes in the table below to complete the explanation of how the Earth was formed.

Cause	Effect
2. Planetesimals accumulated.	
3.	The planet became spherical.
4.	The Earth was made warmer.
5. The inside rock could not cool off as quickly as the temperature increased.	

▲ ▲ **CHAPTER 19**

6. As the rocks of the young Earth melted, the denser, heavier

materials _____ , while the lighter

materials _____ the surface.

7. The sources of energy for heating the Earth were

_____ materials and heat added by

_____ and other falling materials.

Each of the following phrases refers to a layer of the Earth shown in Figure 17. In the space provided, identify each phrase as describing the Earth's *crust*, *mantle*, or *core*.

8. _____ a thin skin over the entire planet

9. _____ contains the heaviest materials, such as iron and nickel

10. _____ the middle layer

11. _____ extends to the center of the Earth

12. _____ inhabited by humans

The Atmosphere Evolves (p. 526)

13. Take a look at the Chemistry Connection in the left column. By studying the chemistry of Titan, scientists hope to

a. figure out how Titan can support human life.
b. understand the formation of nitrogen.
c. learn how molecules essential to life may be formed.

14. Over 4 billion years ago, no life existed on Earth. What else was different about Earth at that time?

_____

_____

15. Fifty years ago, scientists thought Earth's early atmosphere was composed of mostly methane, ammonia, water, and hydrogen

compounds. True or False? (Circle one.)

16. Most of Earth's matter probably came from material similar to

_____ , while the remaining part came

from planetesimals of ice, called _____ .

17. Heated minerals released gases into the Earth's first atmosphere.

True or False? (Circle one.)

18. Which two gases made up the Earth's first atmosphere?

_____

19. Where do scientists think most of the water for Earth's oceans came from?

    a. volcanic gases   **c.** Venus

    b. meteoroids   **d.** comets

Mark each of the following statements *True* or *False*.

20. _____ The gases in the Earth's second atmosphere came only from volcanoes.

21. _____ The ozone layer was much thicker in Earth's early atmosphere.

22. _____ UV light helped form Earth's current atmosphere.

23. How can UV light be dangerous to your skin?

_____

_____

_____

24. _____ produced oxygen through the process of photosynthesis. These organisms were protected from ultraviolet radiation by a layer of _____ .

25. Which of the following events completely changed the Earth's atmosphere?

    a. Comets hit the Earth's surface.

    b. Ultraviolet rays hit bodies of water.

    c. Early life-forms produced oxygen.

Oceans and Continents (p. 529)

26. When did a global ocean cover the planet?

_____

27. Continents have existed since the formation of the Earth.

True or False? (Circle one.)

28. Crust material is heavier than mantle material. True or False? (Circle one.)

CHAPTER 19

29. What does the composition of granite tell geologists about rock in the Earth's crust?

    a. The composition of granite has not changed.

    b. Rocks in the Earth's crust have melted and cooled many times.

    c. The Earth's crust doesn't contain granite.

30. Place the following statements in the correct sequence to explain continent formation by writing the appropriate number in the space provided.

    _____ Cooler, denser materials sank due to gravity.

    _____ Less dense, hot rocks rose to the surface and melted.

    _____ Melted rock erupted through volcanoes.

    _____ The slow convective motion in the Earth's mantle caused the mantle rock to rise and sink.

    _____ Cooler material began to reheat.

31. The continents haven't stayed in the same place since their formation. True or False? (Circle one.)

Review (p. 529)

Now that you've finished Section 3, review what you learned by answering the Review questions in your ScienceLog.

CHAPTER
20 **DIRECTED READING WORKSHEET**

A Family of Planets

As you read Chapter 20, which begins on page 536 of your textbook, answer the following questions.

Imagine . . . (p. 536)

1. Where does the word *planet* come from, and what is its meaning?

_____

_____

2. Which is the largest planet?
    a. Jupiter   **c.** Saturn
    b. Earth   **d.** Neptune

What Do You Think? (p. 537)

Answer these questions in your ScienceLog now. Then later, you'll have a chance to revise your answers based on what you've learned.

Investigate! (p. 537)

3. What is the purpose of this activity?

_____

_____

_____

Section 1: The Nine Planets (p. 538)

4. In 1957, the former Soviet Union launched Sputnik. What was Sputnik?

_____

Measuring Interplanetary Distances (p. 538)

5. The amount of time it takes light to travel around the Earth seven and a half times is _____ .

6. How many light-minutes are there in one astronomical unit?

_____

7. Distances within the solar system must be measured in light-years. True or False? (Circle one.)

The Inner Planets (p. 539)

8. In general, how are the inner planets different from the outer planets? (Circle all that apply.)

   a. They are not spherical.
   b. They are different in size.
   c. They are made of different materials.
   d. They are closer together than the outer planets are.

9. Which group of planets does Earth belong to?

_____

Complete the following section after reading pages 539–543. Be sure to examine the statistics for each planet. Each of the statements refers to an inner planet. In the space provided, write *ME* for Mercury, *V* for Venus, or *MA* for Mars.

10. _____ This is the only planet besides Earth with some form of water.

11. _____ This planet spins in a clockwise direction.

12. _____ This planet has the biggest range in surface temperatures.

13. _____ The largest mountain in the solar system is on this planet.

14. _____ On this planet, the sun rises in the west and sets in the east.

15. _____ This planet has the densest atmosphere of all the inner planets.

16. _____ This planet has the thinnest atmosphere.

17. What is the goal of the Earth Science Enterprise? (Circle all that apply.)

   a. to study human effects on the global environment
   b. to study whether life is possible on Mars
   c. to get away from the Earth
   d. to study the Earth using satellites

Review (p. 543)

Now that you've finished the first part of Section 1, review what you learned by answering the Review questions in your ScienceLog.

The Outer Planets (p. 544)

18. Why are the outer planets called gas giants?

_____

_____

Complete the following section after reading pages 544–548. Choose the planet in Column B that matches the description in Column A, and write the corresponding letter in the space provided. Planets may be used more than once.

Column A	Column B
_____ **19.** Like Jupiter, this planet is composed of hydrogen and helium.	**a.** Jupiter
_____ **20.** This planet is covered by nitrogen ice.	**b.** Saturn
_____ **21.** Its moon is more than half its size.	**c.** Uranus
_____ **22.** This planet may have been tipped over by a massive object.	**d.** Neptune
_____ **23.** The Great Red Spot is on this planet.	**e.** Pluto
_____ **24.** This planet is about 15 times more massive than Earth.	
_____ **25.** This planet's atmosphere contains belts of highly visible clouds.	
_____ **26.** Like Jupiter, this planet gives off more heat than it receives from the sun.	

27. Which three planets were not known to ancient people?

    a. Saturn, Jupiter, and Pluto   **c.** Jupiter, Uranus, and Neptune
    b. Uranus, Neptune, and Pluto   **d.** Mercury, Venus, and Saturn

Review (p. 548)

Now that you've finished Section 1, review what you learned by answering the Review questions in your ScienceLog.

Section 2: Moons (p. 549)

1. What is the difference between a moon and a satellite?

_____

_____

2. Which planets do not have moons?

    a. Mercury and Venus   **c.** Uranus and Neptune
    b. Neptune and Pluto   **d.** Mars and Pluto

Chapter 20, continued

Luna: The Moon of Earth (p. 549)

Mark each of the following statements *True* or *False*.

3. _____ The moon's composition is similar to the composition of the Earth's crust.

4. _____ The rocks brought back from the moon during the 1960s and 1970s are about 4.6 billion years old.

5. _____ The missions to the moon have not given us any information about other parts of the solar system.

6. Before the Apollo missions, which of the following ideas was NOT used to explain the formation of the moon?

   a. It was captured by the Earth's gravity.
   b. It resulted when the Earth was hit by a planet-sized object.
   c. It spun off from the Earth.
   d. It formed independently from the same materials that make up the Earth.

7. Which of the following is NOT part of the current theory about the formation of the moon?

   a. It resulted when the Earth was hit by another object.
   b. It was formed partially from material from Earth.
   c. Some of the craters on the moon formed during a cooling period.
   d. It formed independently from materials different from those that make up the Earth.

8. As a result of the changing positions of the moon relative to the Earth and sun, the moon has different appearances, called

   _____ .

9. Take a look at Figure 23 on page 551. What is the difference between a new moon and a full moon?

   _____

   _____

   _____

10. When the sunlit part of the moon appears to grow larger, we

    say the moon is _____ .
    (waxing or waning)

11. As the moon changes its position relative to the Earth and sun,

    we always see the same side of the moon. True or False?
    (Circle one.)

Chapter 20, continued

Choose the word in Column B that best matches the definition in Column A, and write the corresponding letter in the space provided.

Column A	Column B
_____ **12.** The shadow of the Earth falls on the moon.	**a.** annular eclipse
_____ **13.** The shadow of the moon falls on the Earth.	**b.** lunar eclipse
_____ **14.** A thin ring is visible around the outer edge of the moon.	**c.** solar eclipse

15. During a lunar eclipse, the moon often turns deep blue.

True or False? (Circle one.)

Review (p. 553)

Now that you've finished the first part of Section 2, review what you learned by answering the Review questions in your ScienceLog.

The Moons of Other Planets (p. 554)

16. Phobos and Deimos are moons of Mars. Where do scientists think these moons come from, and why?

_____

_____

_____

_____

_____

17. Ganymede is the largest of Jupiter's 16 moons. It is larger than

   a. Mercury.   **c.** Earth.

   b. Venus.   **d.** Mars.

18. Europa is another of Jupiter's moons. Why do scientists wonder if some form of life might be there?

_____

_____

_____

_____

CHAPTER 20

Complete the following section after reading pages 555–557. Write the number of moons of each planet in the space provided.

19. _____ Neptune

20. _____ Saturn

21. _____ Uranus

22. _____ Pluto

Choose the moon in Column B that best matches the description in Column A, and write the corresponding letter in the space provided.

Column A	Column B
_____ **23.** revolves backward around its planet	**a.** Titan
_____ **24.** hazy orange atmosphere containing nitrogen and methane	**b.** Charon
_____ **25.** patchwork surface of plains, grooves, and cliffs	**c.** Miranda
_____ **26.** period of revolution is 6.4 days long	**d.** Triton

Review (p. 556)

Now that you've finished Section 2, review what you learned by answering the Review questions in your ScienceLog.

Section 3: Small Bodies in the Solar System (p. 557)

1. Name two objects in the solar system besides moons and planets.

_____

Comets (p. 557)

2. What are "dirty snowballs," and why are they given that name?

_____

_____

3. Comets can have more than one tail. True or False? (Circle one.)

4. How are the orbits of comets different from the orbits of planets?

_____

_____

_____

5. Where do comets come from? (Circle all that apply.)

    a. the Oort Cloud   **c.** the asteroid belt

    b. the Kuiper Belt   **d.** an area between Earth and Mars

Asteroids (p. 559)

   6. Where would you most likely find asteroids?

_____

_____

_____

   7. Asteroids have a variety of sizes, shapes, and compositions.

      True or False? (Circle one.)

   8. Asteroids closest to the sun are

    a. rich in carbon.

    b. stony or metallic in composition.

    c. rich in organic matter.

    d. dark gray on their surfaces.

   9. When do scientists think asteroids originated?

_____

_____

_____

Meteoroids (p. 560)

10. What is the main difference between a meteoroid and an asteroid?

_____

_____

_____

Mark each of the following statements *True* or *False*.

11. _____ A meteorite is a meteoroid that enters Earth's atmosphere and strikes the ground.

12. _____ A meteor shower occurs when Earth passes through the dusty debris left behind by a comet.

13. _____ All meteorites are made up of the same types of materials.

14. _____ A meteor is a small, rocky body orbiting the sun.

CHAPTER 20

15. Which type of meteorite may contain organic minerals and water?

   a. stony

   b. metallic

   c. stony iron

Role of Impacts in the Solar System (p. 561)

16. Why does the Earth receive fewer impacts than the moon?

_____

_____

_____

_____

_____

_____

17. Why don't we see many craters on Earth? (Circle all that apply.)

   a. weathering

   b. tectonic activity

   c. small objects burn up in the atmosphere

   d. erosion

18. Many scientists believe that a cosmic impact caused the extinction of the dinosaurs. How often do these kinds of impacts occur?

   a. every few hundred years

   b. every few thousand years

   c. every few million years

   d. every 30 million to 50 million years

Review (p. 561)

Now that you've finished Section 3, review what you learned by answering the Review questions in your ScienceLog.

The Universe Beyond

As you read Chapter 21, which begins on page 568 of your textbook, answer the following questions.

Imagine (p. 568)

1. Robert Williams decided to focus the Hubble Space Telescope on what looked like an empty piece of sky. What did he find?

   _____

   _____

2. You will learn about _____ and the

   _____ they are made of in this chapter.

What Do You Think? (p. 569)

Answer these questions in your ScienceLog now. Then later, you'll have a chance to revise your answers based on what you've learned.

Investigate! (p. 569)

3. Each galaxy contains _____ of stars. (millions or billions)

4. All galaxies are the same shape. True or False? (Circle one.)

Section 1: Stars (p. 570)

5. What is a star?

   _____

   _____

6. To learn more about stars, astronomers study

   _____ .

Color of Stars (p. 570)

7. Place these colors of flame in order from hottest to coolest: red, blue, and yellow.

   _____

8. Astronomers think that stars have different

   _____ because they are different colors.

_____

Chapter 21, continued

_____

Composition of Stars (p. 570)

9. A prism spreads sunlight into its colors. Similarly, a

_____ spreads starlight into its colors.

Mark each of the following statements *True* or *False*.

10. _____ The part of a star we see gives off a continuous
spectrum.

11. _____ Every element has its own set of emission lines.

12. A cool gas _____ the same colors of light

that it would _____ if it were heated.

13. Take a moment to look at the Physics Connection in the right
column of page 571. How do police use spectrographs to identify
cars?

_____

_____

_____

_____

14. A spectrum of starlight taken with a spectrograph is a

_____ spectrum with

_____ lines called an absorption
spectrum.

Classifying Stars (p. 572)

15. Today, stars are classified by temperature. The hottest stars are

   a. yellow.   **c.** red.
   b. orange.   **d.** blue.

16. If a star's spectrum does not contain an absorption line for an
element, then the star cannot contain the element.

   True or False? (Circle one.)

17. Look at the Biology Connection in the left column of page 572.
Why is it hard to distinguish star colors at night?

_____

_____

_____

Look at the chart of the types of stars on page 573 to answer the following questions.

18. Class F stars are

    a. yellow.   **c.** yellow-white.

    b. blue-white.   **d.** orange.

19. Which element is found in the spectra of the hottest stars?

    a. calcium   **c.** iron

    b. hydrogen   **d.** helium

20. The surface temperature of our sun is

between _____ and _____ °C.

How Bright Is That Star? (p. 574)

Mark each of the following statements *True* or *False*.

21. _____ If one star looks dimmer than another nearby in the night sky, it is most likely smaller than the other.

22. _____ A first-magnitude star is brighter than a sixth magnitude star.

23. _____ Apparent magnitude is how bright a star looks in the night sky.

24. The sun's absolute magnitude is 4.8, which is not very high. Why is this star the brightest object in the sky?

_____

_____

Distance to the Stars (p. 575)

25. Light travels about _____ km in one light-year.

26. As Earth revolves around the sun, more-distant stars seem to shift position in relation to stars near the Earth. True or False? (Circle one.)

Motions of Stars (p. 575)

27. At different times of the year, the night side of the Earth faces a different part of the universe. True or False? (Circle one.)

28. Some stars seem to _____ and

_____ because of the rotation of the Earth on its axis.

29. Look at Figure 8. If you could travel through time, would the constellations look the same from Earth 200,000 years in the future as they do now? Explain.

_____

_____

_____

Review (p. 576)

Now that you've finished Section 1, review what you learned by answering the Review questions in your ScienceLog.

Section 2: The Life Cycle of Stars (p. 577)

1. When a star dies, either gradually or in a big explosion, much of

its material returns to _____ .

The Diagram That Did It! (p. 577)

2. An H-R diagram shows the relationships of which of the following? (Circle all that apply.)

a. a star's absolute magnitude
b. a star's apparent magnitude
c. a star's surface temperature
d. a star's velocity

3. An H-R diagram shows how stars can be classified by temperature

and brightness. True or False? (Circle one.)

The H-R Diagram (p. 578)

4. According to the H-R diagram in your textbook, the star Canopus

has a temperature of about _____ and

an absolute magnitude of _____ .

5. Which type of star would you find in the lower right corner of an H-R diagram?

a. a red, faint star
b. a blue, faint star
c. a cool, bright star
d. a yellow, bright star

6. Main sequence stars move _____ and

to the _____ on an H-R diagram as they age. (up or down, right or left)

Choose the type of star in Column B that best fits the description in Column A, and write the appropriate letter in the space provided.

Column A	Column B
____ **7.** stars with low mass, temperature, and absolute magnitude	**a.** massive blue stars
____ **8.** small, hot stars that are dimmer than the sun	**b.** white-dwarf stars
____ **9.** high-temperature stars that are brighter than the sun and that quickly use up their hydrogen	**c.** red giant stars
____ **10.** cool stars with high absolute magnitudes	**d.** red-dwarf stars
____ **11.** stars that are in the band that runs along the middle of the H-R diagram	**e.** main sequence stars

When Stars Get Old (p. 580)

12. Which of the following statements is NOT true of supernovas?

    a. The explosion can be brighter than a galaxy.
    b. The explosion occurs at the beginning of a blue star's life.
    c. Silver, gold, and lead can be produced during the explosion.
    d. After the explosion, the supernova may shine for many days.

13. A supernova explosion was observed on Earth in 1987, but the explosion actually took place about 169,000 years ago. How is this possible?

_____

_____

_____

14. Which of the following statements are true of neutron stars? (Circle all that apply.)

    a. They are only about 20 km across.
    b. They are made up of neutrons.
    c. They are not very dense.
    d. They are the leftover material in the center of a supernova.

15. A pulsar is a neutron star that is spinning. True or False? (Circle one.)

16. Which of the following are true of black holes?
(Circle all that apply.)

    a. They are larger than neutron stars.

    b. Light cannot escape them due to the strength of their gravity.

    c. They have no mass.

    d. Astronomers use X rays to detect their location.

Review (p. 581)

Now that you've finished Section 2, review what you learned by answering the Review questions in your ScienceLog.

Section 3: Galaxies (p. 582)

1. What holds groups of stars, such as galaxies, together?

_____

_____

Types of Galaxies (p. 582)

Each of the following statements is true of a spiral galaxy, an elliptical galaxy, or an irregular galaxy. In the space provided, write *S* for a spiral galaxy, *E* for an elliptical galaxy, and *I* for an irregular galaxy.

2. _____ These galaxies contain only old stars.

3. _____ The Milky Way is probably this type of galaxy.

4. _____ Many of these galaxies may have their gravity distorted by neighboring galaxies.

5. _____ Most galaxies are this type of galaxy.

6. _____ These galaxies are massive blobs of stars.

7. In a spiral galaxy, hot blue stars are located in the

_____ . (spiral arms or nuclear bulge)

Contents of Galaxies (p. 584)

8. Stars are the largest features in galaxies. True or False?
(Circle one.)

9. What do nebulas have to do with new stars?

_____

_____

10. Globular clusters usually contain fewer stars than open clusters.

True or False? (Circle one.)

Origin of Galaxies (p. 585)

11. Why is looking through a telescope like looking back through time?

_____

_____

_____

12. All of the following are true about quasars EXCEPT

    a. quasars are very large.

    b. quasars may be the earliest types of galaxies ever formed.

    c. quasars are very far away.

    d. quasars may have enormous black holes at their center.

Review (p. 585)

Now that you've finished Section 3, review what you learned by answering the Review questions in your ScienceLog.

Section 4: Formation of the Universe (p. 586)

1. The study of the _____ and

_____ of the universe is cosmology.

The Big Bang Theory (p. 586)

2. According to the big bang theory, the universe began 10 billion to

15 billion years ago with a huge explosion. True or False? (Circle one.)

3. If there is enough matter in the universe, it may stop expanding

outward and start collapsing. True or False? (Circle one.)

4. Which of the following is evidence that supports the big bang theory?

    a. stars getting older and becoming dark

    b. background radiation coming from all directions in space

    c. excess amounts of mass in the universe

    d. a large vacuum in space

Universal Expansion (p. 587)

Mark each of the following statements *True* or *False*.

5. _____ Scientists have shown that the Milky Way is near the center of the universe.

6. _____ Almost all of the galaxies in the universe are moving away from all of the other galaxies in the universe.

7. To discover the age of the universe, what do scientists have to know about galaxies?

_____

_____

_____

8. Another way to measure the age of the universe would be to measure the age of the oldest stars in the universe. What has been the problem with this method so far?

   a. Scientists have not found any stars that are very old.

   b. None of the very old stars are close enough to Earth to be accurately measured.

   c. The measurements show that some stars are older than the universe.

   d. The sun is the only star in our galaxy to measure.

Structure of the Universe (p. 589)

Arrange the following structures in order from smallest to largest, with 1 being the smallest, by writing the appropriate number in the space provided.

9. _____ galaxies

10. _____ planets

11. _____ superclusters

12. _____ star clusters

13. _____ galaxy groups

14. _____ planetary systems

15. _____ galaxy clusters

Review (p. 589)

Now that you've finished Section 4, review what you learned by answering the Review questions in your ScienceLog.

CHAPTER

22   DIRECTED READING WORKSHEET

Exploring Space

As you read Chapter 22, which begins on page 596 of your textbook, answer the following questions.

This Really Happened! (p. 596)

1. How far away were instruments able to pick up shock waves from the Florida launch of *Saturn V?*

_____

_____

Investigate! (p. 597)

2. How does a rocket work?

_____

_____

_____

What Do You Think? (p. 597)

Answer these questions in your ScienceLog now. Then later, you'll have a chance to revise your answers based on what you've learned.

Section 1: Rocket Science (p. 598)

3. How did Jules Verne send his fictional character to the moon?

_____

_____

The Beginning of Rocket Science (p. 598)

4. American physicist _____ is considered to be the father of modern rocketry.

From Rocket Bombs to Rocket Ships (p. 599)

5. *V-2* rocket designer Wernher von Braun and his entire research team surrendered to the Americans near the end of World War II.

True or False? (Circle one.)

6. Why was NASA formed?

_____

_____

_____

How Rockets Work (p. 600)

7. State the principle of physics that explains how rockets work.

_____

_____

8. _____ is the force that accelerates a rocket.

9. In Figure 4, the hot gases in the _____ chamber are under high pressure.

10. For a rocket to move skyward, what must become greater than the weight of the rocket?
  a. the weight of the air pushing under the rocket
  b. the force of the gas exiting at the bottom of the rocket
  c. the force of the gas pushing at the top of the combustion chamber

11. A rocket must reach a speed of 8 km/s in order to break away from Earth's gravitational pull. True or False? (Circle one.)

12. Why must rockets carry oxygen when traveling into space?

_____

_____

_____

_____

Review (p. 601)

Now that you've finished Section 1, review what you learned by answering the Review questions in your ScienceLog.

Section 2: Artificial Satellites (p. 602)

1. The Soviet Union launched an artificial satellite before the United States did. True or False? (Circle one.)

Chapter 22, continued

The Space Race Begins (p. 602)

Choose the satellite in Column B that is described in Column A, and write the corresponding letter in the space provided.

Column A	Column B
____ **2.** a satellite that carried a dog	**a.** *Sputnik 1*
____ **3.** the first artificial satellite to successfully orbit the Earth	**b.** *Explorer 1*
____ **4.** discovered the Van Allen radiation belts	**c.** *Sputnik 2*

Into the Information Age (p. 603)

5. *Tiros 1* was the first United States weather satellite.

True or False? (Circle one.)

6. The first United States _____ satellite was *Echo 1*.

Choose Your Orbit (p. 603)

7. What is LEO?

a. limited Earth orbit   **c.** low Earth orbit
b. low emission orbit   **d.** low Earth operation

8. How does a satellite in geosynchronous orbit (GEO) help with your television's reception of a program?

_____

_____

_____

_____

_____

_____

_____

Results of the Satellite Programs (p. 604)

9. Using satellites, scientists have been able to obtain information

by _____ sensing—gathering images and data from high above Earth's surface.

10. Because the Cold War is over, the United States no longer needs to use spy satellites for military defense. True or False? (Circle one.)

11. According to the Environment Connection on page 604, what branch of the military tracks "space junk"?

_____

_____

_____

12. What have remote-sensing projects, such as Landsat, allowed scientists to do? (Circle all that apply.)

   a. simplify mineral exploration
   b. map the lunar surface
   c. look at changes in growth patterns of vegetation
   d. study the effect of humans on the global environment

Review (p. 605)

Now that you've finished Section 2, review what you learned by answering the Review questions in your ScienceLog.

Section 3: Space Probes (p. 606)

1. The golden era of space exploration took place in the

_____ and early

_____ .

2. What is the difference between a space probe and a satellite?

_____

_____

_____

_____

Visits to Our Planetary Neighborhood (p. 606)

Mark each of the following statements *True* or *False*.

3. _____ The first space probe was launched by the Soviets.

4. _____ *Luna 3* made the first soft landing on the moon.

5. _____ *Clementine* discovered evidence of water on the moon.

Chapter 22, continued

6. What have we learned about Venus from space probes? (Circle all that apply.)

   a. The surface rocks are very different from those on Earth.
   b. The temperature and atmospheric pressure are very high.
   c. The planet has mountains and volcanoes.
   d. Some type of plate tectonics takes place.

Choose the Mars space probe from Column B that best matches the description in Column A, and write the corresponding letter in the space provided. Probes may be used more than once.

Column A	Column B
____ **7.** deployed *Sojourner*	**a.** *Viking 2*
____ **8.** looked for signs of life on Mars	**b.** *Mars Pathfinder*
____ **9.** designed to use less-expensive technology to study the Martian surface	
____ **10.** found evidence that Mars once had a warmer and wetter climate than it does today	

11. *Pioneer 10* and *Pioneer 11* sampled the flow of particles coming

   from the sun called _____ .

12. State the name of the first space probe to leave our solar system and the year it left.

   _____

   _____

13. What are two of the exciting things that *Galileo* has discovered about Jupiter's moons?

   _____

   _____

   _____

Space Probes—A New Approach (p. 610)
14. What is NASA's new approach to space probes?

   _____

   _____

   _____

Mark each of the following statements *True* or *False*.

15. _____ The *Stardust* will collect material from the tail of a comet and return the material to Earth.

16. _____ NASA is no longer testing any risky technology.

17. What is so unusual about the method of propulsion used in *Deep Space 1?*

_____

_____

_____

18. The *Cassini* probe is being sent to Saturn to tour the planet's system of moons. True or False? (Circle one.)

19. Which of the following is NOT a proposal for a future condensed mission into space?

   a. a space-probe visit to the sun
   b. an orbiter for Europa
   c. an orbiter for Mercury
   d. a space-probe visit to Pluto

Review (p. 611)

Now that you've finished Section 3, review what you learned by answering the Review questions in your ScienceLog.

Section 4: Living and Working in Space (p. 612)

1. The goal of the Mercury program was to put a man on the moon.

   True or False? (Circle one.)

Human Space Exploration (p. 612)

2. The first human to orbit Earth was Soviet cosmonaut

_____ , in the year

_____ .

3. Why was John F. Kennedy's announcement about sending a man to the moon such a surprise?

_____

_____

_____

4. The first human to set foot on the moon was American

    Neil Armstrong, in the year 1972. True or False? (Circle one.)

5. What did the crew of *Apollo 11* bring back from the moon?

    _____

    _____

The Space Shuttle (p. 613)

6. Which of the following does NOT describe a space shuttle?

    a. It is a reusable vehicle.
    b. It lands like a helicopter.
    c. It takes off like a rocket.
    d. It is manned.

7. How did the explosion of the *Challenger* affect the space shuttle program?

    _____

    _____

Space Stations—People Working in Space (p. 614)

8. The world leader in space-station development was the former

    _____ . The United States benefited from
    this space station program by learning more about the effects of

    _____ on the human body.

9. Why did *Skylab* fall into the ocean?

    _____

    _____

    _____

    _____

    _____

    _____

    _____

10. Only Russian cosmonauts have been allowed to work on the *Mir*

    space station. True or False? (Circle one.)

11. Which of the following have NOT been conducted on *Mir?*

   a. studies of manufacturing technologies in space
   b. astronomy experiments
   c. observations of Earth's orbit
   d. All of the above have been conducted on *Mir.*

The International Space Station (p. 616)

12. How is the International Space Station being assembled?

_____

_____

_____

_____

The Moon, Mars, and Beyond (p. 617)

13. What will be the key to colonizing the moon?

   a. making colonization economically worthwhile
   b. using helium in nuclear reactors
   c. establishing recreational uses
   d. developing more technology

Review (p. 617)

Now that you've finished Section 4, review what you learned by answering the Review questions in your ScienceLog.